D1717635

Governing Farmer Rehabilitation and Resettlement in India

Dissertation

**zur Erlangung des akademischen Grades
doctor rerum agriculturarum
(Dr. rer. agr.)**

**eingereicht an der
Lebenswissenschaftlichen Fakultät
der Humboldt-Universität zu Berlin**

von
Vikram Patil, M.Sc.
geboren am 26. Juni 1984 in Hoskoti, Karnataka, India

Präsident der Humboldt-Universität zu Berlin
Prof. Dr. Jan-Hendrik Olbertz

Dekan der
Lebenswissenschaftlichen Fakultät
Prof. Dr. Richard Lucius

Gutachter: 1. Prof. Dr. Dr. h.c. Konrad Hagedorn
             2. Prof. Dr. Vinish Kathuria

Tag der mündlichen Prüfung: 02.09.2015

Institutional Change in Agriculture and Natural Resources
Institutioneller Wandel der Landwirtschaft und Ressourcennutzung

Governing Sustainability in India

edited by/herausgegeben von
Volker Beckmann & Konrad Hagedorn

Volume/Band 61

Vikram Patil

Governing Farmer Rehabilitation
and Resettlement in India

Shaker Verlag
Aachen 2015

Bibliographic information published by the Deutsche Nationalbibliothek
The Deutsche Nationalbibliothek lists this publication in the Deutsche
Nationalbibliografie; detailed bibliographic data are available in the Internet at
http://dnb.d-nb.de.

Zugl.: Berlin, Humboldt-Univ., Diss., 2015

ISBN 978-3-8440-4092-0
ISSN 1617-4828

Shaker Verlag GmbH • P.O. BOX 101818 • D-52018 Aachen
Phone: 0049/2407/9596-0 • Telefax: 0049/2407/9596-9
Internet: www.shaker.de • e-mail: info@shaker.de

Aim and Scope of the Series

„Nothing endures but change". Heraclitus the Ephesian (ca. 535–475 BC)

Institutions, defined as "the rules of the game", are a key factor to the sustainable development of societies. They structure not only the multitude of human-human interactions of modern societies, but also most of the human-nature interactions. Poverty, famine, civil war, degradation of natural resources and even the collapse of ecosystems and societies often have institutional causes, likewise social and economic prosperity, sustainable use of resources and the resilience of socio-ecological systems. Agriculture, forestry and fisheries are those human activities where the interdependencies between human-human and human-nature interactions are perhaps most pronounced, and diverse institutions have been developed in history to govern them.

Social and ecological conditions are, however, ever changing, which continuously challenge the existing institutional structure at a given point in time. Those changes may be long-term, like population growth or climate change, medium-term, such as new technologies or changing price relations, or short-term, like floods or bankruptcies, but all of them pose the question whether the rules of the game need to be adapted. Failures to adapt timely and effectively may come at a high social cost. Institutional change, however, face a principal dilemma: on the one hand, institutions need to be stable to structure expectations and effectively influence human behaviors; on the other hand, they need to be adaptive to respond to the ever changing circumstance mentioned above. Understanding stability and change as well as developing adaptive institutions and effective, efficient and fair mechanisms of change are, therefore, of central importance for societies and an ongoing research challenge for social scientists.

If we want to improve the effectiveness, efficiency and adaptability of institutions, it stands to reason that we have to develop a good understanding of the causes, effects, processes and mechanism of stability and change. This is the aim of the series "Institutional Change in Agriculture and Natural Resources," which attempts to answer the questions "How do processes and mechanism of institutional change actually work? What and who are the main determinants and actors driving, governing and influencing these processes? What are the economic, political, social and ecological consequences? How can adaptive institutions be designed and developed, and what governance structures are required to make them effective?" These are the questions at the heart of the series. The works published in this series seek to provide answers to these questions in different economic, social, political and historical contexts.

Volker Beckmann and Konrad Hagedorn
Ernst-Moritz-Arndt-Universität Greifswald und Humboldt-Universität zu Berlin

Focus of the *Governing Sustainability in India* subseries

Deep transformations of interconnected social, ecological and technical systems are taking place in many regions of the world, requiring complex processes of institutional change. In India, such processes of transformation are particularly intense. As in many other countries, the main drivers there can be found in population growth associated with demographic change and economic growth, closely interlinked with technological change. Especially in Indian society, this often occurs in contexts of high population density, extreme resource scarcity, weak carrying capacity of ecosystems and harmful pollution. The growing economy calls for reliable energy provision and increased energy efficiency while, at the same time, also needing to cope with climate change.

The ICAR subseries Governing Sustainability in India provides a collection of studies on such action situations in both rural and urban areas. Rural areas are increasingly affected by the above-mentioned problems, as people's livelihoods there often depend directly on well-functioning bio-physical systems. They suffer from soil erosion, declining water tables, loss of biodiversity, impacts of climate change and other crucial problems. In Indian cities meanwhile, particularly its emerging megacities, urbanization is proceeding rapidly, leading to increased demand on natural resources. Changing lifestyles and economic growth are increasing energy consumption and greenhouse gas emissions. Climate change impacts, worsened by such urban developments, are already causing extreme weather events such as floods, heat waves and droughts.

In such action situations, crafting institutions can be the key to achieving sustainable development. The young researchers presenting their analyses in this subseries have accepted this challenge and engaged in excellent, in-depth studies. A variety of related issues were analysed, including enhanced energy efficiency, power-generation efficiency, policies for renewable energy, political discourses for promoting biofuels, sustainable traffic solutions, sustainable food chains, localized food systems, food accessibility for the urban poor, electricity provision for irrigation, microcredit organisations to combat poverty, governance of water allocation, industrial water pollution abatement, collective action in watershed management, rehabilitation of displaced farmers, and local service delivery. We are very grateful to the authors for having employed well-developed analytical frameworks, enlightening theoretical approaches and multiple methods to contribute to our common knowledge base. They have been working together with many partners in India and elsewhere, to whom we also want to express our special gratitude.

Volker Beckmann and Konrad Hagedorn
Ernst-Moritz-Arndt-Universität Greifswald & Humboldt Universität zu Berlin

Acknowledgements

Like others, I also started my PhD with immense enthusiasm to work for economic issues and contribute to frontline research. However, obstacles were many and without the help of advisors and peers the journey would not have been successful. Swami Vivekananda said that, in a day, when you do not come across any obstacles, you can be sure that you are traveling in a wrong path. I express my foremost gratitude to Professor Konrad Hagedorn for his excellent guidance, constant support, close counsel, and valuable suggestions throughout my doctoral studies. I confess that it has been a rare privilege to be under his guidance. I thank him for providing all the facilities to carry out my research. I gratefully extend my gratitude to Professor Vinish Kathuria for his similar support and encouragement. He has been truly an exemplary mentor to me, without whom it would have been difficult to complete my thesis by this time. Not only his scholarly research guidance, but also his keen interest, and patience have inspired me to work hard and complete this seemingly never ending task. I also extend my gratitude to Professor MG Chandrakanth for his constant encouragement and support.

My introduction to and inspiration for the world of institutional economics were mainly through thoughtful teachings of Daniel Bromley, Konrad Hagedorn, and Kate Farrell. I was also privileged to have gained research skills from inspirational teachings of many professors during the doctoral certificate courses, especially Thomas Heckelei, Ulrich Koester, Bernhard Brümmer and Vera Bitsch. I am also thankful to participants and organizers of the following conferences and summer schools: RSSIA 2014 – Russia (Moscow), HIP workshop 2014 – Germany (Berlin), GEWISOLA 2013 – Germany (Berlin), ICAE 2012 – Brazil (Foz do Iguaçu), ICAE 2015– Italy (Milan), and LANDac 2015 – the Netherlands (Utrecht). I acknowledge the funding assistance of RSSIA, ICAE 2012 and 2015.

I am very fortune to have great friends and colleagues at Humboldt University who extended their constant support during each and every step of this wonderful journey. I am grateful to Ranjan Ghosh for his support and counseling in both my academic as well as personal life. Without his constructive ideas and suggestions, and his patience towards my silly arguments, I would have not achieved this progress up to now. I am very thankful to Christine Werthmann for her feedback and support while designing my proposal and initial fieldwork. I am also grateful to Majunath AV for his support especially while applying for the IPSWaT scholarship and building my research proposal at the beginning of my Ph.D. I extend my thanks to Julian Sagebiel for his fruitful discussion and constructive   feedbacks while designing the choice experiment. I am also thankful to other colleagues from RESS especially Jens Rommel, Srinivas Reddy Srigiri, Kate Farrell, Sergio Villamayor-Tomas, Philipp Grundmann, and Andreas Thiel for their feedback. I would also like to thank my friends Mario Torres, Kiran Kumar MN, Keerthi Kiran, Divya, Saikumar, Monish, Gayatri, Nitya, Ravi, and others for their direct and indirect support. My special appreciation also goes to Sigrid Heilmann, Ines Jeworski, and Renate Judis for their constant help and support all along this journey. I am indebted to them for their constant care and concern. My sincere gratitude to the farmers and the UKP officials for their cooperation during the fieldwork. My special thanks to Chetan, Toufeeq, and Balesh, who assisted me for my fieldwork. I also thank my friends Sadasiv, Vittal, Prashanth, Vikas and Allamaprabhu for extending their helping hands during my research stay. I am also very thankful to my friends who filled the gaps in my life before and during this journey: Timmanna and his wife Shridevi, Mohankumar KG and his wife Mamatha.

This work is dedicated to my entire family but first and foremost my parents. I would like to express my deep gratitude to my parent-in-laws, my brothers Vasudevsutadas and Vivekanand Patil, my sister Radha Mullur, my brother-in-law Krishna Mullur, my sister-in-laws Savita Patil and Manjula Donur, my nephews Jagannath and Shrihari, nieces Sachchi Devi and Navinya, my sister Reema Priya and especially my wife Kavita Patil, and my little daughter Vasudha.

I also dedicate this work to all my gurus who are my inspiration and motivation: Radhanath Swami, Bhakti Rasamrita Swami, Gaur Gopal Das, Vasudevsuta Das, Gopesh Prabhu, Priya Govinda Das, Konrad Hagedorn, Vinish Kathuria, PG Kulkarni, MG Chandrakanth, and SS Ganti. I greatly appreciate the financial support from IPSWaT program – International Postgraduate Studies in Water Technologies and Erasmus Mundus IMRD. Finally, I offer my gratitude to those who are unintendedly missing in this brief acknowledgement.

Berlin, June, 2015   Vikram Patil

Table of Contents

List of Figures

List of Tables

List of Abbreviations

CA	Consent Award
CLS	Complete Land Submergence
CMSR	Centre for Management and Social Research
DIDR	Development Induced Displacement and Rehabilitation
DSR	District Schedule of Rates
EIA	Environmental Impact Assessment
FGDs	Focus Group Discussions
FRL	Full Reservoir Level
GA	General Award
GoI	Government of India
GoK	Government of Karnataka
IGS	Income Generating Scheme grant
IoS	Institutions of Sustainability
IVPROBIT	Instrumental Variable Probit
KBJNL	Krishna Bhagya Jala Nigam Ltd.
KRPDPA	Karnataka Resettlement of Project Displaced Persons Act
LAA	Land Acquisition Act
LPG	Land Purchase Grant
MLA	Member of Legislative Assembly
mm	Millimeters
MRD	Ministry of Rural Development
MW	Mega Watt
NGOs	Non-Government Organizations

NIE	New Institutional Economics
NPRR	National Policy for Resettlement and Rehabilitation
NRP	National Rehabilitation Policy
PACs	Price Advisory Committees
PLS	Partial Land Submergence
R&R	Rehabilitation and Resettlement
RFCTLARR	Right to Fair Compensation and Transparency in Land Acquisition, Rehabilitation, and Resettlement Act
ROLM	Rank-Ordered Logit Model
RRBs	Regional Rural Banks
SCs	Scheduled Castes
SIA	Social Impact Assessment
SLA	Special Land Acquisition
STs	Scheduled Tribes
TCE	Transaction Cost Economics
TISS	Tata Institute of Social Sciences
TMC	Thousand Million Cubic
UKP	Upper Krishna Project

1 Introduction

Land is a prime input for development projects. High demand for land is a paramount issue especially in developing world. Because, on the one hand, population density is on the rise, and on the other, many development projects are being implemented to meet the growing needs of increasing population. Development projects like dams and irrigation, road and rail infrastructure, urbanization, special economic zones, and industrialization are mushrooming in order to achieve economic growth and development. Such projects are inevitable for generating employment, increasing food production, and to meet the other growing needs. They, however, also impose risks of irreversible social, economic, cultural, and environmental consequences on some sections of the population. This is because such projects require involuntary acquisition of large number of individuals' private property rights in land, which implies displacement from their economically, socially, and culturally deep rooted locations.

Each year, around 10-15 million people are involuntarily displaced as a consequence of development projects worldwide (Stanley 2000). This calculation excludes a large number of unaccountable and minor projects' displacement, inclusion of which will raise the figures of displaced. Dams and irrigation projects are one of the major contributors to development induced population displacement (Stanley 2000; Robinson 2003). Each year they alone contribute around 40 per cent to the total population displacement by the development projects (Stanley 2004). This accounts for about population of 5-6 million. Displacement due to World Bank irrigation projects, which are active during the year 1993, accounts for 66 per cent (13 million) of total population displaced (Stanley 2000). Among the total displacement in the World Bank projects across the world that are active in the year 1993, a significant contribution (52 per cent) is in South Asia, in which India is the largest country involving many irrigation projects (Stanley 2000; Robinson 2003).

As of now, there are more than 5000 large dams, which have been built or are being built in India (GoI 2013). Since independence, it is estimated that approximately 60 million people have been displaced in India due to development projects, out of which 40 per cent are tribal (Choudhury 2013). However, according to the Ministry of Rural Development (1996) and Shah (2010) this number is not only underestimated, but laws on land acquisition have not been very successful in rehabilitating and resettling the displaced people. Unlike in the developed world, acquisition of land for development projects in a country like India requires displacement of a large mass of population because, land holding is very much fragmented and involves many landowners. In addition, as agricultural activities are more labor intensive, livelihood of many landless peasants depend on these land holdings. Hence, issues of land acquisition and displacement have become prominent. As a result, project-induced displacement of people is one of the major contentious issues in economic development of India (Choudhury 2013).

Risks of post-displacement disruptions of communities involved in development projects is a major challenge in institutionalizing and governing land acquisition and Development-Induced Displacement and Rehabilitation (DIDR) of people. Until recently, the issues of institutionalizing the land acquisition in general, and governance processes of overall process of DIDR and people's preferences towards compensation in particular are overlooked. Hence, economic analysis of land acquisition and DIDR domain of development projects from the perspective of institutional economics has not received a great deal of attention. This thesis, using an ongoing irrigation project in India, makes an attempt to examine the institutional and governance challenges of land acquisition and DIDR of people. That ongoing project is called the Upper Krishna Project (UKP).

1.1 Development Challenges in the Study Area

The UKP is being implemented across the river Krishna in the northern region of the state of Karnataka in India. Due to historical negligence and natural limitations, north Karnataka is economically underdeveloped. The low and erratic rainfall pattern, high day temperatures, and semiarid climatic factors limit agricultural productivity. In India, alongside Rajasthan, Karnataka possesses the largest drought prone area with 70 per cent of the geographical area being arid and semiarid. These form 15 per cent and 3 per cent respectively of the total semiarid and arid regions of India (Nagaraja et al. 2010). Within the state of Karnataka, the northern region is the most drought prone area. The provision of adequate infrastructure, education, and health facilities has still remained a challenge in the area even after successive attempts of the government. With large arid areas, poverty and consecutive acute drought spells have exacerbated the predicament. About 60 per cent of the state's poor and 66 per cent of the *taluks*[1] facing poverty are located in this region of Karnataka (GoK, 2011). Although agriculture is the main source of income for the people in this region, it is characterized by low productivity. On the other hand, 90 per cent of the population is dependent on agriculture for their livelihood (Nagaraja et al. 2010). The distinguishing features of north Karnataka from the rest of the state and India are shown in Table 1-1. Bijapur, Bagalkot, Bidar, Gulbarga, and Raichur are the districts of northern Karnataka, which comprise the semi-arid zone with low and erratic rainfall and high evapotranspiration. The average annual rainfall ranges from 400 to 750 millimeters with a moisture index[2] between -33 and -60 per

---

[1] *Taluk* is an administrative division under the district governing a town and villages under its jurisdictions. This is similar to counties in US or *Amt* in Germany.

[2] The moisture index is that portion of the total precipitation used to satisfy plant (vegetation) needs, which is an overall measure of precipitation effectiveness for plant growth

cent (Ramachandra et al. 2004). These districts are situated in the rain-shadow[3] area with frequent spells of drought. Agriculture in this area is mainly rain-fed although there is some surface irrigation from its various river belts.

Table 1-1: Distinguishing features of North Karnataka, Karnataka and India, 2011-12

Sl. No	Particulars	North Karnataka	Karnataka	India
1	Per Capita Income (Rs.)	46865	89545	74920
2	Literacy (%)	64.93	75.60	74.04
3	Average Annual Rainfall (mm)	600	1151	1083
4	Working population dependent on Agriculture and Allied Activities (%)	90.00	55.80	53.20

Source: (GoI 2011d; World Bank 2014; GoI 2014a; KoI 2015b)

1.2 The Upper Krishna Project

The Krishna river is an inter-state river passing through three states of India namely Maharashtra, Karnataka, and Andhra Pradesh. The river inflow is very high during the monsoon and low during the summer. In order to regulate the wide fluctuation of the river and provide irrigation to the farmers throughout the year, the government of Karnataka (GoK) proposed an irrigation project called the Upper Krishna Project (UKP) in the year 1963, which is currently one of the largest irrigation projects in Asia. The UKP is a multipurpose project in India, and is planned to be implemented in three stages (Jaamdar 2006). In Stage I (1963-1997), two dams - Almatti and Narayanpur - along with associated canal and lift irrigation schemes were built, where 138 villages were displaced completely (Table 1-2). In Stage II (1997-2000), remaining canal and lift irrigation schemes were completed, where 41 villages and nearly half of district town of Bagalkot were displaced. Stage III is in the process of implementation, where storage capacity of the Almatti dam will be increased from 519.60 meters to 524.26 meters. In order to complete this stage, 22 villages will be displaced. The UKP got complete funding assistance from the central government and the

---

(AMS 2012). Negative figures indicate the high evapotranspiration and low moisture availability.

[3] Rain-shadow area is an arid or semi-arid region, where rainfall is hindered by mountain ranges that disrupt the structure of cyclones passing over the region and by the presence of greatly heated land surfaces (Salem 1989).

World Bank. The World Bank assistance was 24.28 per cent and 21.35 per cent
of the total cost in stage I and stage II respectively (GoK 2004). Due to uncertainty of the World Bank's future support, the GoK subsequently established a
government owned company called the Krishna Bhagya Jala Nigam Ltd.
(KBJNL) to borrow and mobilize the required funds from the domestic bond
market. However, the Asian Development Bank (ADB) has assured a part of
funding for the final stage. The objectives of the project are to bring the drought
prone rain-fed area under irrigation to increase agricultural production, farmers'
income, and employment as well as to generate power.

**Table 1-2: Village and population displacement due to Upper Krishna
            Project**

Sl. No	Stage and phase of the UKP	Number of villages submerged	Total population displaced
1	Stage-I Phase-I	43	50,000
2	Stage-I Phase – II	95	270,000
3	Stage-II	41 + 1*	80,000
4	Stage-III	22	87,576
	Total	**201 + 1***	**487,576**

Note:* Bagalkot Town
Source: Upper Krishna Project III Action Plan I (KoI 2006)

The project provides irrigation to the four drought prone districts of north Karnataka, namely Bagalkot, Bijapur, Raichur and Gulbarga (Jaamdar 2006;
Tribunal 2010). In the first stage of the project, it was estimated to provide irrigation to approximately 425,000 hectares of land. In the second stage, the storage capacity of the Almatti dam was increased by raising its full reservoir level
(FRL) to 519.6 meter to utilize further quantum of 54 thousand million cubic
(TMC) feet of water for providing irrigation to an additional extent of 197,000
hectares (*ibid.*). In the ongoing last stage, it is proposed to utilize further 130
TMC of water by raising the FRL of the reservoir to 524.26 meter (*ibid.*). Table
1-3 shows the detailed features of the project. Upon completion of the entire
UKP project providing a FRL of 524.256 meter, it is estimated to provide irrigation to 833,600 hectares of agricultural land (Jaamdar 2006). It is also proposed
to generate power of about 150 megawatt (MW). The Almatti and Narayanpur
dams with all the irrigation canals are perceived as one single project called the
Upper Krishna irrigation project and it is utilizing 442 TMC of the Krishna river
water (*ibid.*). The third stage has been approved, yet is to be implemented in

coming years. While the UKP provides irrigation to a large area and thus bene-fits the farmers living in the *command area*[4], as discussed above, it also displac-es a large number of farmers in the *catchment area*.[5] Construction of both Al-matti and Narayanpur dam along canal and lift irrigation schemes has led to ac-quisition of 105,006 hectares of land affecting 201 villages and 400,000 people of 100,000 families (Jaamdar 2006; Tribunal 2010; GoK 2013b) (Table 1-2). In the final stage, much more land is going to be submerged affecting even greater numbers of people. Due to this, many farmers have been or will be displaced from the affected area. They are compensated with monetary compensation for their lost land and houses through DIDR program.

Table 1-3: Features of Upper Krishna Irrigation project (Stage I & II)

Sl. No	Particulars	Units
1	Total land acquisition in project (Hectares)	105,006
2	Power generation (MW)	150
3	Dam height (meter)	524.26
4	Reservoir capacity (TMC)	442
5	No. of villages displaced	201
6	Total number of families affected	100,000
7	Estimated area to be irrigated	833,600

Source: Author's compilation from various sources of government documents

1.3 Post-displacement Impacts of Upper Krishna Project

The initial plan of the project had the sole purpose of irrigating drought prone districts of northern Karnataka. Later, by adding a power generation component, the UKP became a multipurpose project. This conversion has resulted in in-creased complexities of project implementation, with escalation in project ex-penditure, submergence area, and adversaries of displaced people (Jaamdar 2006). During the early stages of the project (1960-1980s), the government

---

[4] "Command Area" means an area irrigated or capable of being irrigated either by gravita-tional flow or by lift irrigation or by any other method, under an irrigation system, project or source and includes every such area whether it is called "ayacut" or by any other local name in any law in force in the State (GoI 2007a).

[5] A catchment is an area of land that collects water, which drains to the lowest point in the area, which could be a lake, a dam, or the sea. Rain falling on the land will make its way to this lowest point, via creeks, rivers and storm water systems (WHO; UNEP et al. 1997).

hardly emphasized the DIDR domain of the project (*ibid.*). Displaced farmers received only very low monetary compensation in early stages of the project and a few studies confirm that they impoverished with post-displacement low income (Parasuraman 1996; Cernea 1998; World Bank 1998; Jaamdar 2006). Studies also show that young displaced people who have become landless after displacement migrated to larger cities for employment in construction and other branches (Parasuraman 1996). After the late 1980s, widespread awareness about the failure of DIDR programs and post-displacement negative impacts led to many amendments of the institutional arrangements in the DIDR domain of development projects across India and, subsequently, in the UKP as well. In the later stages of the project until now, in order to reestablish displaced farmers' livelihood and regain income foregone due to the shift in their private property rights over land, the GoK has used both provisions - compensating the farmers with monetary and non-monetary provisions. Other compensation provisions include sites for construction of houses, free transport facility to carry their materials to the newly allotted place, land purchase grant and stamp duty[6] exemption, skill development programs, and job reservation for children of displaced farmers. However, some studies found out that some of these provisions did not materialize properly and thus failed to reach intended farmers (GoK 2013b).

In spite of DIDR reforms with both monetary and non-monetary compensation provisions in the UKP, a post-displacement evaluation study done by Tata Institute of Social Sciences (TISS), Mumbai, shows that affected people faced severe problems and were impoverished after their displacement (UKP Committee 2004; Jaamdar 2006). The UKP documentation committee (2004) reported that the standard of living and social status of displaced farmers deteriorated after displacement. Small farmers and landless farmers among the displaced farmers were most seriously affected by the displacement. As farmers became landless, the number of landless increased and found difficulty in getting employment post-displacement. As a result most of these farmers migrated to nearby towns or larger cities in search of employment in construction and other works (Parasuraman 1996). Hence, the GoK failed in providing adequate resources and in enhancing their abilities to regain their livelihoods (UKP Committee 2004).

1.4 Apportionment of Monetary Compensation

For the apportionment of monetary compensation, like elsewhere in India, there are two alternative compensation-claiming methods. The first is called 'consent award' (CA) where farmers agree with the compensation amount decided under

---

[6] Stamp duty is a tax collected by a government that is levied on those instruments or documents of transactions when selling and buying property, like bills of exchange, cheques, promissory notes, bills of lading, letters of credit, policies of insurance, transfer of shares, debentures, proxies and receipts (GoI 2011e; Anonymous 2015; GoK 2015a)

the CA and give formal consent to the government that they will not approach for judicial arbitration in future for higher compensation. After the consent, farmers receive the compensation amount within a short period. In case of the UKP, the Price Advisory Committees formed by the GoK in 1996 estimated the base value of land. That is, the value of land by taking into account the previous registered sales deeds and several other factors that affect land prices in the vicinity. Then, additional 30 per cent of the base value as solatium[7] and 12 per cent as additional market value along with the base value is paid as total compensation under the CA. This method of valuation has been chosen in order to match with prevalent market value in the vicinity (GoK 2006). Normally, registered values of voluntary land transactions are much lower than the market values. This is because landowners deliberately report the land price low while registering land transactions to avoid stamp duty (Vyas and Mahalingam 2011; Singh 2012).

The second compensation claiming method is called 'general award' (GA), an alternative specialized dispute settlement award, which has a low initial compensation and a scope for judicial arbitration for higher compensation. Hence, farmers have the right to approach the court for higher compensation claim in this award. In the GA, the initial compensation is equal to the average registered value of previous three years land transactions in the vicinity. Landowners are compensated by the amount that is decided in the arbitration plus an interest amount for the entire period of litigation. The average arbitration time noticed in the UKP is five to six years. Table 1-4 compare the two awards based on several features. Both the awards have advantages and disadvantages in terms of opportunity costs, transaction costs, and total amount of compensation claimed. However, farmers are free to opt for either of the mechanisms based on their individual preferences. In terms of total compensation claimed, the GA provides an incentive to farmers to get higher compensation than the CA (World Bank 1998; Singh 2012). Yet, it is observed that the majority of the farmers displaced due to the UKP so far claimed the compensation through the CA in spite of the fact that they have an incentive to get higher compensation through the GA.

1.5 Problem Statement

Involuntary displacement of people is implicit in the process of most of the developmental programs. Many DIDR programs of public infrastructure projects in developing countries often face a variety of impoverishment risks and institutional challenges in rehabilitation of displaced people especially vulnerable who

---

[7] An enhanced/extra compensation premium paid due to the compulsory nature of the acquisition to cover unseen effects / non-financial disadvantage due to displacement from his or her original place as a result of acquisition, like lack of access to common places and natural resources, increased distance from the land, disturbed social capital, etc. (World Bank 1998).

usually do not have the power and voice (Cernea 1997; Mathur 2006a). The displaced are often already poor and might end-up worse off for a long period after displacement (Cernea 1997; Kanbur 2003; Serageldin 2006). In this process, people face complex socio-economic problems (De Wet 2006a). This is mainly because of the weak institutional arrangements and the ineffective enforcement mechanism in rehabilitation of the displaced people (Mathur 2006a). The sustainability of livelihoods and distribution equalities of benefits depends on the institutions of the DIDR of the people (*ibid.*). Studies have found that the standards of living of many displaced farmers, especially those of small and marginal farmers as well as of agricultural laborers, have deteriorated after their displacement (Parasuraman 1996; Mathur 2006a; Singh 2012). Although the government has reformed the institutions of DIDR, the majority of farmers have become marginalized and/or even landless after the involuntary resettlement (Parasuraman 1996; World Bank 1998). They were thus not able to keep their original per capita income and standards of living. The research question therefore we ask is "why have institutional arrangements and governance structure of the DIDR failed to achieve desirable outcome of rehabilitation?" This thesis attempts to answer this through institutional analysis of land acquisition and DIDR.

Table 1-4: Characteristics of compensation claim awards – consent award vs. general award

	Consent Award	**General Award**
Transaction cost	Low to both landowners and the government	High to both the parties
Scope of arbitration	No	Yes
Claiming process	Quick (6 months)	Lengthy (average 5-6 years)
Third party influence	Government officials	Lawyers
Total compensation	Less compensation as compared to the GA	Comparatively high total compensation
Initial compensation	High	Low

Source: Own Compilation

A particular drawback of most of the studies done so far is their lack of consideration of institutional reform process associated with land acquisition and DIDR of people. Hence, the central focus is to investigate the governance of the DIDR and the farmers' *access* to either of the compensation claim mechanisms.

The newly enacted Right to Fair Compensation and Transparency in Land Acquisition, Rehabilitation, and Resettlement (Amendment) Ordinance 2015 ensures the participation of local actors in the process of land acquisition for development projects. The bill also has the provision of taking the consent of 70 to 80 per cent of land owners when the government acquires land and compulsory job provision clause. Given these provisions, the study also investigates those farmers, who are going to be displaced due to the on-going final stage of the project, for their preferences towards compensation. With this background, I identified three issues in overall process of land acquisition and DIDR, namely i) governance deficits of the DIDR of people, ii) compensation mechanisms to acquire land and other immovable assets, and iii) farmers preferences towards compensation provisions if their participation is allowed in the decision making of the DIDR.

In order to investigate these issues, three different but coherent approaches of institutional analysis are adopted using the elements posited by Institutions of Sustainability (IoS) framework (Hagedorn 2008), namely, transaction cost theory, access-based property rights and institutional fit. Here intended actors are displaced farmers who have lost or are going to lose their land, houses, and other immovable assets. The action situation implies land acquisition and DIDR. Contemporary institutional arrangements of DIDR are compensation claiming mechanisms, the CA and the GA. The primary goal of this dissertation is to gain a deeper understanding of how the actors (the displaced farmers) behave in the action situation given the institutional arrangements of DIDR, what characteristics of actors influence such a behavior, and how the governance structures influence an outcome of the transaction? The dissertation further investigates what are the preferences of concerned actors (farmers) for the means of achieving an outcome. The outcome (of DIDR) is rehabilitation of the displaced farmers through restoring their economic activities, physical dwelling facilities, and intact socio-cultural environment.

Therefore, this thesis initially explores how and why farmers are further marginalized after displacement given the institutions and governance structure of DIDR as a whole. This question is addressed at two levels: the governance level, which refers to the organization of entire rehabilitation process, and the actors' level which includes farmers' decision making associated with numerous interactions with various other actors. At the governance level, a comparative analysis of governance structures of DIDR is done by using a transaction cost economics (TCE) perspectives. Based on the TCE concept of discriminative alignment, I frame the hypothesis that the current form of organizing DIDR incurs high transaction cost and post-contractual hazards to displaced farmers. Farmers do not have information about *ex-post* uncertainties and opportunities before the involuntary land transaction and thus, become marginalized after displacement. Then, at actors' level, the issues of access to either of the compensation claim mechanisms by using access based property rights redistribution theories are analyzed. The guiding hypothesis is that those farmers having access mechanisms are able to choose the GA and get higher compensation. This hypothesis is tested using a dichotomous choice model to analyze the primary data collected from 199 displaced farmers. The results help us better understand why displaced farmers are further marginalized in contemporary mode governing DIDR in the development projects.

Subsequently preferences of the farmers, who have not been yet displaced but will be eventually displaced, are analyzed. A choice experiment is conducted in order to analyze farmers' preferences towards compensation provisions. Here, the hypothesis is that, given the farmers' characteristics and local situation, there is a mismatch between the provisions of contemporary institutional arrangements of DIDR and farmers expectations. Farmers would prefer other alternatives like land-based and employment-based compensation provisions compared to the *status quo* monetary compensation provisions. Hence, the objectives of the study can be summarized as follows.

1.6 Research Objectives

As mentioned above the main research question of the study is why have institutional arrangements and governance structure of the DIDR failed to achieve desirable outcome of rehabilitation? The current research work contributes to this question, first, by studying the institutional reforms in the DIDR of development projects. Then the role of governance processes in marginalization of the displaced farmers and determinants of the farmers' decisions makings towards compensation claim methods are analysed. Finally, farmers' preferences towards different compensation options are analysed in order to understand the gap between the provisions of the contemporary DIDR framework and farmers' expectations. Thus, the main research objectives are:

1. To study the institutional reform process of land acquisition and DIDR.

2. To analyze the role of governance issues in marginalization of the displaced farmers given the contemporary institutional arrangements of the DIDR.

3. To analyze the factors determining the choice of either of the two compensation mechanisms and the role of actors' characteristics in this decision making.

4. To analyze farmers' preferences for different DIDR alternative options.

1.7 Thesis Structure

The preliminary hypothesis is that the desirable performance of institutional arrangements and governance structures depend on how well they match with local conditions and actors, and how efficient the governance structure organizes DIDR related transactions. This is explored in the following chapters from various theoretical and empirical perspectives. The dissertation is organized as follows:

Chapter 2 describes the evolution of institutional arrangements for land acquisition and DIDR in development projects of India. This is done in order to understand how the institutions have evolved over the years in India in general and in the UKP in particular. In addition, there is a lack of in-depth research on rehabilitation problems from the institutional economics perspectives. To address the research questions mentioned above, analytical and theoretical foundations are laid down in Chapter 3. This chapter explores the IoS framework and presents an understanding of the elements of institutional analysis of nature related transactions (here in this study, land) and link between them. In order to address these elements of the IoS framework, theories like transaction cost theory, access based property rights approach and the concept of institutional fit are employed. These theoretical foundations help in identifying suitable variables that can be employed to empirical investigation of the remaining objectives of the study. The governance deficits of rehabilitation is presented in Chapter 4, where it is argued that the government, by allowing the farmers in open market to re-purchase the land, imposes high transaction costs on them and there are *ex-post* hazard in land market. As a result, a majority of the farmers ends up not owning comparable assets after their displacement and thus getting further marginalized. Hence, the contemporary mode of governance is inefficient in rehabilitating the farmers. Chapter 5 presents an analysis of the factors that determine the choice of either of the two compensation mechanisms of contemporary DIDR institutional arrangements. The role of farmers' characteristics such as social and physical capital, information and knowledge, and political bargaining power on their decision making is analyzed. Results indicate that the decision is governed by access to political bargaining power (in terms of wealth, political affiliation, and network) and information. Therefore, farmers lacking these fail to get the benefits from the GA, which further creates distributional inequalities among the displaced farmers.

Chapter 6 deals with the question of what farmers prefer towards alternative DIDR options. A choice experiment is conducted in order to examine this question. Using the farmers' preference for compensation options as an indicator of social fit, it is argued that the current institutional arrangements of DIDR are misfit as there is mismatch between farmers' expectation and the status quo provisions of DIDR. This is because of *ex-post* risks of monetary compensation farmers face due to their limited capabilities and portfolio management skills. The results validate this hypothesis, as the majority of farmers preferred land-and employment-based compensation provision. Therefore, from all three empirical investigations, it is implied that institutions matter but need to be contextualized. These results have important policy implications and prescribe farmers' participation in decision making. Finally, Chapter 7 concludes with the insights from the previous chapters of the thesis, general policy implications, and a discussion on further scope of research.

2 Institutional Evolution of Land Acquisition and Rehabilitation

Overview

Institutional arrangements for land acquisition and rehabilitation of displaced people play a crucial role in governing sustainable rehabilitation and resettlement (R&R). Organization and performance of the R&R is directly correlated with the presence of domestic or national institutions of development-induced displacement and rehabilitation (DIDR) (Cernea 2006). Hence, this chapter provides an overview of institutional reforms of land acquisition and rehabilitation. It also briefly highlights the provisions of rehabilitation program and the procedure undertaken in land acquisition, displacement, and rehabilitation of farmers. Until recently there was no law as such for the R&R of displaced people in India[1] (Mathur 2006a). This absence of institution(s) during six decades of development and growth post-independence is a major cause of the R&R failures in India (Cernea 2006; Mathur 2006a). In such situations, displaced people, with limited capabilities, were unable to tackle and adapt to the post-displacement social and economic disruptions (Mathur 2006a). Due to the disruptive nature of involuntary displacement and its growing awareness, people's outrage has grown leading to opposition, protests, and movements against such displacement (Cernea 2006; Mathur 2006a; Serageldin 2006). The Narmada river valley project[2] is one such large project, which resulted in nationwide protests; this not only brought widespread awareness but also exerted pressure on the government to provide prominence to this issue. In order to deal with such issues, the government introduced several reforms. Such institutional reforms of rehabilitation are explained in this chapter. By taking into consideration the complexity involved in the land acquisition and rehabilitation, the provisions and the general procedure of the R&R is also explained. This chapter provides a basis for empirical investigations of the thesis to follow.

---

[1] There was no national law to govern rehabilitation, during which rehabilitation was under the provisions of the LAA 1894 or project specific provisions laid by donor agencies or state governments.

[2] The Narmada river valley project is one of largest multipurpose development projects with 30 large, 135 medium, and 3000 small dams on the river Narmada, that passes through three states of India, Madhya Pradesh, Maharashtra, and Gujarat. The extent of displacement due to this project is 51,447 families across 244 villages (Garikipati 2005; NCA 2015).

2.1 Institutional Arrangements for Land Acquisition and Rehabilitation in India

2.1.1 Post-independence Reforms of Land Acquisition Act 1894

After independence, as discussed in previous chapter, a large number of large infrastructure development projects, mainly irrigation and transportation, have been implemented in India in order to achieve growth and economic development that led to displacement of a large population in many places across the country. Consequently, many people have been affected due to expropriation of their land and displacement. Until recently, the Land Acquisition Act (LAA) 1894 (including amendments) was the general law for acquisition of land and amount of compensation for affected people (GoI 1894). Nevertheless, the provisions of the LAA focus more on the acquisition process with little emphasis on the R&R of displaced farmers. This lack of attention to the R&R has led to many conflicts between the government and the citizens, especially farmers and environmentalists (Ministry of Rural Development 1996; Asif 1999; Iyer 2007; Desai 2011). The main points of contention are: improper compensation and rehabilitation of displaced people, acquisition of fertile land, and environmental problems involved in implementing development projects. As a result, projects like the Sardar Sarovar Dam in the state of Gujarat, the Omkareshwar Dam in Madhya Pradesh, the Hirakud Dam in Orissa, the Tata Nano Singur project in West Bengal, the Bangalore-Mysore Infrastructure Corridor project in Karnataka and many others have faced domestic resistance through protests and movements (Nayak 2010; Ray 2010). Subsequently, external funding agencies (like the World Bank) for some of these development projects threatened the government with withdrawing funding in absence of reforms in land acquisition and R&R process. In response to this threat, some states like Karnataka, Maharashtra, Rajasthan, and Madhya Pradesh began to frame their individual state level rehabilitation policies with the assistance of external funding agencies. This led to further criticism with the vociferous claim for a national law to adequately deal with the issues of rehabilitation of displaced people. Thereafter, several amendments in the LAA 1894 and project-specific institutional arrangements began to emerge gradually.

The LAA 1894 is an old British colonial Act which was enacted in 1894 in order to acquire privately owned land and to maintain law and order (Mathur 2006a). This act provides the government unilateral power to acquire land and other immoveable assets whenever needed for public purpose. The clause 'public purpose' under the LAA 1894 is often criticized because of ambiguity of its definition and its misuse (Fernandes 1998; Mathur 2006a; EPW 2011; Singh 2012). In return for loss of land and houses, people were entitled only to a modest monetary compensation as per the Act. The power of the state to acquire land and other properties without or with minimum compensation was then restricted through the Constitution (seventeenth amendment) Act 1964 (GoI 1964; Das 2006). This amendment gave land owners the right to claim higher compensation. In addition, a provision was made to provide 15 per cent of total compensation as solatium. However, displaced people were seriously neglected in implementation process of such projects, which further led to criticisms of the LAA 1894 by both national experts and international donor agencies.

Subsequently, the Government of India amended the LAA 1894 in 1967 and then in 1984 in order to fasten the acquisition process and provide comparable compensation amount to displaced people (GoI 1984; Das 2006). The changes made in 1984 were mainly in order to protect the affected people. Major changes included assignment of a time frame to complete the acquisition process (1-2 years depending on type of projects), enhancement of solatium from 15 per cent to 30 per cent of total compensation, payment of 12 per cent interest rate from the date of notification till the date of award, and clear definition of the clause 'public purpose'(Das 2006). In spite of these changes, the Act continued to attract criticism because of lack of proper enforcement mechanism and participation of affected people in the decision making process (Ministry of Rural Development 1996; Desai et al. 2007; Vyas and Mahalingam 2011). Hence, the Act suffered from delays in processing, evaluation of compensation, acquisition, weak bureaucracy, complexities and conflicts involved in the acquisition and compensation process (Asif 1999; Reddy and Reddy 2007; Dash 2009; Ranganathan 2010; Bose 2013; Sampat 2013). This was the only act until recently to acquire individual and community-owned land and other immoveable assets for public purpose development projects.

Since compensation is not sufficient to buy comparable assets, Mathur (2006b) pointed out that income restoration programs are not included in the rehabilitation policy. Initially, solely the government used to decide on the compensation amount and affected people had no option but to accept it. This unilateral way of land acquisition and compensation distribution is generally criticized as being highly undemocratic. As a result, the government introduced a judicial arbitration system where farmers, when not satisfied with the amount compensated, are entitled to approach a court for a higher compensation claim. Both the central and the state governments subsequently proposed the following amendments to the LAA 1894 (Saxena 2006):

i) 'Land for land' compensation for tribal people

ii) Landless farmers and other affected people should be given certain minimum amount of compensation

iii) Affected people should be informed about the detailed R&R plan so as to bring more transparency

iv) The principle of market value should be replaced with replacement value while deciding on the compensation amount

v)   The solatium should be increased to 100 per cent of compensation as
      against current 30 per cent

vi)   Consultation of affected people prior to acquisition through conducting
      village meetings (Gram Sabhas).

Later on, some states like Karnataka, Maharashtra, Rajasthan and Madhya Pradesh also made their individual state level rehabilitation policies with the assistance of external funding agencies (Mathur 2006a). However, most of them either failed to enforce these changes or enforced them with hardly any commitment (Mathur 2006a; Saxena 2006).

2.1.2 National Rehabilitation Policy

The Government of India (GoI), Ministry of Rural Development (MRD), thus
began a policy drafting process in the early 1990s. According to Cernea (2006),
this has been long overdue mainly because of a lack of commitment and throw-
ing the ball of legal responsibility on each other between states and central government. Subsequently, the GoI promulgated the National Policy on Resettlement and Rehabilitation (NPRR) for project-displaced families in 2004 (GoI
2004). The provisions of the NPRR were to place emphasis on a proper compensation method either in terms of land or in terms of money. Further, it focused
on the R&R of affected farmers so as to ensure that their original standard of living remains. The provisions also include the minimization of displacement as far
as possible, to ensure the protection of the rights of the weaker sections of the
society (Saxena 2006). The GoI amended the NPRR in 2006 and the result was
the National Rehabilitation Policy (NRP) 2006 (GoI 2006). The GoI again revised the NRP in 2007 and renamed it as National Rehabilitation and Resettlement Policy (NRRP) 2007 (GoI 2007b). The major amendments in the NRRP
2007 were:

i)   The compulsory undertaking of a Social Impact Assessment (SIA), an
      Environmental Impact Assessment (EIA) and a baseline survey by the
      project before the process of acquisition of land and implementation of
      the project

ii)   Providing additional benefits beyond the monetary compensation to the
      affected people including landless laborers

iii) Providing a timeframe within which the project should provide
      compensation

iv)   Rehabilitate affected people and utilize acquired land for the specified
      reason

v)   Minimize displacement to the maximum extent possible

vi)   Consultation of affected people

vii) Creating job opportunities

viii) Gender Neutrality

ix) House for House

x) Land for all agricultural families

xi) Basic amenities at the new site.

Even after the NRRP 2007 and multiple amendments to the LAA 1894, there has been heightened public concern on land acquisition, especially for multi-cropped irrigated land. Several studies criticized the framework provided by the LAA 1894 due to the perversities inherent in its provisions (Fernandes 1998; Asif 1999; Das 2006; Saxena 2006; Pandey and Morris 2007; Ramaswamy 2009; Desai 2011; Bagchi 2012). These perversities include: lack of transparency in the acquisition process and non-participation of affected communities, improper rehabilitation packages, weak enforcement mechanism, lack of sanctioning for non-compliance, ignoring the preferences and rights of the land owners, unfair acquisition and valuation, and insufficiency and inadequacy of the monetary compensation. Due to this, the government of India took a very long time to develop suitable amendments to the LAA and R&R policy in balancing the need for land requirement for developments projects and protecting the interests of the affected people. By integrating the LAA 1894 and the NRP 2007, the GoI, very recently, drafted "the Land Acquisition, Rehabilitation and Resettlement (LARR) bill 2011" (GoI 2011c). The legislation aimed to address concerns of farmers and those whose livelihoods are dependent on the land being acquired, while at the same time facilitating land acquisition for industrialization, infrastructure, and urbanization projects in a timely and transparent manner. The basic prescription of the bill is as follows:

"A bill to ensure a humane, participatory, informed consultative and transparent process for land acquisition for industrialization, development of essential infrastructural facilities and urbanization with the least disturbance to the owners of the land and other affected families and provide just and fair compensation to the affected families whose land has been acquired or proposed to be acquired or are affected by such acquisition and make adequate provisions for such affected persons for their rehabilitation and resettlement thereof, and for ensuring that the cumulative outcome of compulsory acquisition should be that affected persons become partners in development leading to an improvement in their post-acquisition social and economic status and for matters connected therewith or incidental thereto" (Standing Comittee Report on LARR 2012).

The provisions of the bill include the preparation and appraisal of the SIA study by an expert group, the constitution of a committee to examine proposals for land acquisition and the SIA report, special provisions to safeguard food security, notification and acquisition of land, the R&R award, apportionment of compensation and land for land compensation in case of irrigation projects especially to those belonging to scheduled castes and scheduled tribes[3].

Very recently, the bill has been renamed and enacted with slight modifications as "The Right to Fair Compensation and Transparency in Land Acquisition, Rehabilitation, and Resettlement (RFCTLARR) Act 2013" (GoI 2014b). However, this act has undergone severe criticisms because many projects held up due to some of its clauses, especially taking consent from 70 to 80 percent of the farmers in the area for land acquisition (NDTV 2013a; 2013b, 2013c; Sud 2014; J.O'S. 2015). The new government came up with some revisions and additions, and renamed it as "The Right to Fair Compensation and Transparency in Land Acquisition, Rehabilitation and Resettlement (RFCTLARR) (Amendment) Ordinance 2015 (GoI 2015b). The key differences between the RFCTLARR Act 2013 and the RFCTLARR (Amendment) Ordinance 2015 are: i) exemption of some projects from the application of provisions of Chapter II and Chapter III of the RFCTLARR Act 2013 is made in the RFCTLARR (Amendment) Ordinance 2015. These provisions are Social Impact Assessment, prior consent of at least 70-80 per cent of affected families in case private companies acquisition for public purpose, and no multi-cropped irrigated land to be acquired.

The projects to be exempted from these provisions are projects vital to national security or defense of India, rural infrastructure including electrification, affordable housing, and housing for poor, industrial corridors set up by the appropriate Government and its undertakings, infrastructure projects including projects under public-private partnership. ii) compulsory provision of employment in either government or private companies to at least one person in each affected family. The other key differences between the LAA 1894, the RFCTLARR 2013, and the RFCTLARR (Amendment) Ordinance 2015 are shown in Table 2-1.

---

[3] The Scheduled Castes (SCs) and Scheduled Tribes (STs) are official designations assigned to communities that are historically disadvantaged and backward in social, educational and economics aspects in India (GoI 2015a).

Table 2-1: Key features of old colonial and new acts of land acquisition and rehabilitation

Sl. No	Features	Land Acquisition Act 1894	The Right to Fair Compensation and Transparency in Land Acquisition, Rehabilitation, and Resettlement Act 2013	The Right to Fair Compensation and Transparency in Land Acquisition, Rehabilitation, and Resettlement (Amendment) Ordinance 2015
1	Monetary compensation	As per the registered values of land	Two times the market value of land in Urban areas and Four times the market value in rural areas	Two times the market value of land in urban areas and four times the market value in rural areas
2	SIA	No	Compulsory	Compulsory*
3	EIA	No	Compulsory	Compulsory*
4	Job provision	No	5 % reservation in certain lower categories' jobs of government departments	Compulsory provision of job, either in private or government sectors.
5	Income generating skill development	No	Yes	Yes
6	Public purpose	Nomenclature was vague	Defined and certain type of public projects kept out of this Act	Most of the public projects included
7	Consent from land owners	No	70-80 % of land owners	70-80 % *
8	Share of benefits in urban development projects	No	No	20 percent
9	Private hospitals and educational institutions	No	Excluded	Included
10	Application of R&R provisions	Only public purpose	Pubic purpose & private companies	Public purpose and private companies
11	Solatium	15-30 %	100 %	100 % of total compensation
12	Land for Land (Only in irrigation projects)	No	Min. one acre in command area	Min. one acre in command area

Note: Excluded for certain public projects like defense, rural infrastructure including electrification, affordable housing, and housing for poor, etc.

Source: Author's compilation using Land Acquisition Act 1894, The Right to Fair Compensation and Transparency in Land Acquisition, Rehabilitation, and Resettlement Act 2013, and The Right to Fair Compensation and Transparency in Land Acquisition, Rehabilitation, and Resettlement (Amendment) ordinance 2015.

2.2 Institutional Reforms of Land Acquisition, and rehabilitation and re-settlement in Upper Krishna Project, Karnataka

The broad provisions and procedures followed in the rehabilitation process of almost all the development projects in India are more or less similar, obviously because they are complying with the LAA 1894. However, slight modifications are made in accordance with a particular context and particular projects. The Upper Krishna Project (UKP) has also broadly followed the same provisions, which are under the LAA 1894 but with slight modifications in different phases according to existing situations. The UKP was started in early 1960s. While implementing the UKP stage I until 1980s, as mentioned above, the LAA 1894 with amendments of 1967 was the only general law for the acquisition of land and compensation to be provided to displaced people. In the course of the UKP's implementation, the World Bank as the external funding agency wanted to withdraw its funding commitment (World Bank 1998; GoK 2004; Jaamdar 2006). Reasons for this were, at the one hand, that the Karnataka government had failed to follow the World Bank's rehabilitation guidelines and, on the other hand, it was lacking its own R&R policy. As a result, the people who lost their land and house were hardly cared for (Jaamdar 2006). The threat of withdrawal by the World Bank worked and the Government of Karnataka (GoK) subsequently developed its own R&R package with assistance of the World Bank. In addition to the provisions of monetary compensation, the subsequent R&R package of the GoK also comprised the allocation of land suitable for cultivation to displaced farmers from Almatti and Narayanpur reservoir areas. However, this provision did not materialize due to a lack of appropriate land for reallocation (GoK 2004).

During early stages of the project, some displaced farmers were compensated by land for cultivation wherever government lands were available (Jaamdar 2006). Earlier, the GoK had allocated forest lands to several farmers affected by other projects. However, with the Forest Conservation Act 1980, forest lands became unavailable for being allocated to displaced farmers (GoK 2004). From mid-1980s, the government started compensating the farmers with monetary payments along with some solatium. Hereafter liberalization of the R&R approaches began to emerge. Subsequently the GoK prepared a draft bill called "The Karnataka Resettlement of Project Displaced Persons Bill 1987" in order to adopt a uniform policy for the R&R for the remaining Stages of the UKP (II & III) and all other projects in Karnataka. The GoK published the bill as "Karnataka Resettlement of Project Displaced Persons Act (KRPDPA) 1987"(*ibid.*). The main provisions of the act include apportionment of compensation payable to displaced persons under the LAA 1894, resettlement of displaced persons, extent of land to be granted to displaced persons, occupancy price, and public notice calling upon the displaced persons to state if they want lands for the resettlement (*ibid.*). However, the government decided not to notify the UKP under this Act, as there was a delay in obtaining the assent of the constitutional head of the country, i.e. the President of India.

At this stage, the World Bank had approved the funding for subsequent stages of the project. The Bank, before actually granting the fund, studied the findings of post-displacement evaluation report of the early stage of the project, which showed poor outcomes of the R&R of the displaced people. It demanded to develop better R&R policies and programs and insisted on complying with its own guidelines. However, construction works like raising the height of Almatti dam and construction of canals were done very quickly. Meanwhile, the government of Karnataka ignored the implementation of the R&R component of the project. As a result, the World Bank suspended funding from November 1992 to February 1993 for further implementation processes. This forced the GoK to accept R&R conditions of the World Bank in order to abandon the suspension of funding (Jaamdar 2006). Those conditions are creation of a separate agency to implement the R&R programs, evaluation of affected persons by an independent consultant, provision of extra housing grant and other provisions (*ibid.*).

However, implementation of the R&R did not progress as expected. Due to this mismatch between guidelines and actual implementation of the R&R by the government, the World Bank once again suspended the next tranche of its funding to the project. As a result, land acquisition and R&R implementation of the UKP became major issues in the project implementation. In addition, the World Bank fixed a deadline to complete all the works of the UKP by the year 2000 (Gulati et al. 2005). The GoK sensed the need for an autonomous body in order for funding to be reapproved, raise required additional funding, and complete all the works including land acquisition and R&R before the deadline. Against this background, the Krishna Bhagya Jala Nigam Ltd. (KBJNL) was established with revised guidelines in 1994. This reform was successful in re-approval of funding by the World Bank, raising additional funds required to complete the project, materializing land acquisition and R&R (*ibid.*). The details of fundraising achievements are presented in the appendix (Figure 2-1, Figure 2-2, and Figure 2-3). However, the outcomes of the R&R are much below expectations (Jaamdar 2006).

2.3 Process of Land Acquisition, Displacement, and Rehabilitation and Resettlement in Upper Krishna Project

The Karnataka government established the KBJNL, which is entirely state-owned, in 1994 whose main responsibility is to plan, investigate, estimate, execute, operate, and maintain all the UKP-related irrigation projects. The company is also responsible for land acquisition, the R&R of displaced people, distribution of water and collection of revenues from the users including individual farmers, groups of farmers, towns, city municipalities and industries (Gulati et al. 2005). More specifically, it is responsible to ensure that the following R&R benefits reach the farmers:

- Compensation for submerged land

- Income generating schemes

- Housing grants and free house plots in the resettlement centers for all displaced families including landless laborers

- Transportation of the belongings of the affected families free of costs

- Subsistence allowance for the families in the new locations for the first six months

- Additional housing plots to two major sons and the never-married major daughters of the displaced family

- Vocational training and five percent job reservation in certain categories of government departments

- Waiver of stamp duty on purchase of land / house

- Free ration to the family in the first month of displacement are officially claimed to be provided in the course of resettlement.

The KBJNL has a formal procedure to be followed in the R&R, which is in general a standard procedure also to be followed elsewhere in India. It first forms a committee to conduct baseline surveys of the notified areas / villages of submergence. Then the committee, comprising civil engineers, social scientists and other staff, measures and evaluates land, houses, and other immovable assets of the farmers. The committee writes a report and submits it to the district collector. The district collector then sends the notification about submergence of houses and land to all farmers who are going to be displaced. Notably, the land value in the particular notified village is calculated on per acre basis based on the highest registered value of land in the vicinity. The calculated total compensation is transferred to individual accounts of the farmers. As explained in details in Section 1.4, there are two methods for farmers to claim their monetary compensation – Consent Award and General Award – either of which they are free to opt. Before the actual displacement begins, rehabilitation centers, basic infrastructure like roads, drainage, streetlights, bus stations, electricity, public toilets, schools, and temples are supposed to be constructed.

2.3.1 Survey and Notification of Land and Villages

Before actually starting the land acquisition process, a Full Reservoir Level (FRL) survey of the Reservoirs using 3D Lidar[1] technology is conducted by the jurisdictional irrigation engineers. The survey measures the amount of land and number of villages to be submerged when water is stored at the dams' fullest level. Surveys of land required for construction of dams, network of canals, roads and rehabilitation centers are also done. The survey is conducted twice in order to minimize errors. Upon the completion of the survey, land and villages to be submerged are notified. The requisition proposal, along with survey num-

---

[1] Lidar (Light Detection and Ranging) is an active remote sensing technique that collects very dense and accurate elevation data across landscapes, shallow water areas, and project sites.

bers, specific maps and boundaries, is sent to higher authorities, i.e. the land acquisition officers of respective jurisdictions. The total amount of land, names and number of villages to be acquired, the purposes for and the period within which land is required are also mentioned in the proposal. Regarding the acquisition of houses and other structures, engineers also include the details in the proposal like locations, numbers of local governing body, plinth area, nature of buildings and other details. Finally, the highest authority, the special Deputy Commissioner, approves the proposal after making necessary corrections. Once the proposal is approved, an independent agency is assigned for a socioeconomic survey of people of the villages to be submerged.

2.3.2 Socioeconomic Survey

Once the survey of the FRL and the notification of area are completed, a socioeconomic survey of village people that come under submergence is conducted by an independent agency. Detailed household surveys of each and every family in all the notified villages are conducted. The socioeconomic survey comprises details about family size and structure, education, income sources, immoveable asset holdings like land, house, and other structures, moveable asset holdings like livestock assets, farm implements, and other household items. The socioeconomic survey is necessary to understand the economic status of farmers, which helps in framing the rehabilitation package. Based on the socioeconomic survey, a comprehensive action plan for the R&R is prepared under the R&R guidelines of the government from another independent agency and necessary inclusions are made. Expert opinions from hydrologists and other scientists are also included in order to consider the long- and short-term flood cycles while notifying the area under submergence.

2.3.3 Acquisition of Land and Immoveable Structures and Compensation

After the area and the villages to be submerged are notified and the socioeconomic survey is completed, there are three stages that are followed to acquire land and houses and compensate for their loss.

(i)   Issue of Section 4(1) Notification

Once the requisition proposal of land and village acquisition is approved by the special Deputy Commissioner, a preliminary notification under Section 4(1) of Land Acquisition Act 1894 is made public through four different publication modes. Namely, i) public notice in the concerned village, ii) in two local daily newspapers of regional language, iii) notice to each of the known persons having interest in the land or structures, and iv) in the official gazette of the State Government. The date of publication of latest among these four ways is considered as the date of publication. After this, a period of thirty days is given for affected people, if they have any objections, to respond to the Special Land Acquisition (SLA) officer. During this period, land, house, and other immoveable structures are measured one more time and are verified by all the concerned departments like Survey and Settlement, Irrigation and Revenue.

(ii)   Issue of Section 6(1) Notification

The SLA Officer then prepares and sends the draft declaration proposal under Section 6(1) to the Special Deputy Commissioner. He verifies the declaration proposal and forwards it to the government of Karnataka for its approval. The government verifies if there are any modifications to be made and then approves the draft. After this approval, the draft is published as final declaration under Section 6(1) in four different publication modes as it is followed in the preliminary notification (Section 4(1)). This should happen within a year after the last date of 4(1) notification. Hereafter, the tasks of implementation are delegated to the commissioner (R&R and Land Acquisition) of the UKP.

(iii)   Valuation of Land, Houses and other Immoveable Structures

After the approval and issue of the final declaration by the government, the special land acquisition officer begins the process of valuation of land and other immoveable structures. The officer, in order to minimize the errors, once again verifies the properties to be acquired and begins an enquiry for deciding on the compensation amount. The notices are issued to the owners under the Section 9(1) and 10 of the LAA 1894 and their objections, claims, and request for apportionment are heard. Price Advisory Committees (PACs) consisting of different experts are formed for valuation of land, houses and other immoveable structures. At the time of valuation of the compensation award, the Consent Award (CA) is invoked under Section 11(2) of the LAA 1894. The CA is a provision of compensation based on the mutual discourse and consent between owners and the SLA officer, where owners agree for compensation amount fixed by the PAC and give formal consent to the government that they will not approach court for further higher compensation. The compensation amount in the CA consists of a basic compensation fixed based on the prevailing market value, 30 per cent of market value as solatium, 12 per cent additional market value and interest rate to the market value in case of delay in compensation payment. For the first year, 9 per cent interest is paid and 15 per cent for subsequent years. If the owners do not agree to the compensation amount fixed in the CA, they are free to opt for the General Award (GA), where owners are initially compensated only with basic compensation and they are allowed to approach court for further higher compensation. In the GA, 12 per cent interest rate for a period from notification until the compensation decision is paid along with the compensation amount decided in the court.

A PAC under the chairmanship of the respective Divisional Commissioner decides on the compensation rates for lands to be acquired under the CAs. The structure of the committee is constituted as follows:

   i.   Divisional Commissioner of the Revenue Division – Chairman

   ii.   Special Deputy Commissioner of the jurisdiction - Secretary

   iii. Deputy Commissioner of the district - Member

   iv. Assistant Commissioner of the Sub-division – Member

   v.   District Registrar – Member

   vi. Joint Director of Agriculture – Member

   vii. Representative of Irrigation Department – Member

  viii. Member of Legislative Assembly (MLA) of the area – Member

   ix. A representative of the project displaced farmers' organization - Member.

By taking into account the prevailing market rates and the transaction statistics from the sub-registrar offices of respective vicinities as on the date of or prior to the publication of 4(1) notification, the compensation amount for land is decided on by the PAC separately for dry land, irrigated land with single crop, and with double / perennial crops. Basic fixed compensation for land has been revised few times in the UKP by taking into consideration increases in land price over a period of time and farmers' demand for an increased amount of compensation (Table 2-2). The revised basic compensation in the year 2007, as compared to an order dated in 1998, has been increased by 95 per cent for dry land, single crop land, and double crop land.

A separate committee consisting of engineers, scientists, and bureaucrats is formed to evaluate houses, trees and other immoveable structures based on the district schedule of rates (DSR). The DSRs are the annual prices/rates of inputs/materials of construction of houses and any other structures. For instance, prices of iron, steel, cement, wood, paints, etc. in that particular year are considered. The State Water Resources Department fixes the DSRs annually. Same procedure of invoking the CA is followed while evaluating the houses and other immoveable structures also. The option of the GA is also available in case of acquisition of houses and other immoveable structures. Evaluation of trees, horticultural crops, and agricultural crops are made as per the techno-economic norms of the Forest Department, the Horticultural Department, and the Agricultural Department respectively.

Table 2-2: Revised basic land compensation amounts over a period of time

Sl. No	Type of land	Compensation (Rs. per acre)
I	**As on order dated: 19.06.1998**	
	Dry land	54,000
	Wet land	
	Single crop	90,000
	Double crop	114,000
II	**As on order dated: 21.07.2001**	
	Dry land	70,200
	Wet land	
	Single crop	117,000
	Double crop	148,200
III	**As on order dated 03.01.2007**	
	Dry land	105,300
	Wet land	
	Single crop	175,500
	Double crop	223,300

Source: Adopted from UKP Implementation Report (GoK 2008).

After evaluation of the land, houses, and other immoveable structures including trees and plantations, SLA officer prepares a draft award and forwards it for approval of the authority specified by the government. Under the LAA 1894 a maximum period of two years from the last date of notification under Section 6(1) is specified to complete the award process.

2.3.4 Allocation of House Plots and Displacement

Village meetings (known as Gram Sabhas) are conducted to take into account the opinion of people in deciding about the rehabilitation centers. The rehabilitation center is an area where new village structures are built and house plots are allotted to displaced people. Based on a consensus with the farmers through village meetings, specific areas nearby the displacement site are selected for the establishment of rehabilitation centers. Before actually allotting the house plots to the farmers, the notified area is surveyed and basic infrastructures like formation of layouts, roads, electricity, water supply, drainage, schools, grave yards, bus station, hospitals, temples, community hall, etc. are established. Once the notified area is prepared with these facilities, the house plots are allotted to the farmers based on their land holding before acquisition (Table 2-3).

Table 2-3: Distribution of housing plots based on land holding

Sl. No	Land holding (Hectare)	House plot size (Square meter)
1	Less than 0.25	100
2	0.26 to 3.50	200
3	3.51 to 6.75	300
4	More than 6.75	400

Source: adapted from GoK Report (2006)

2.3.5 Subsidiary Compensation Provisions of Rehabilitation Program

Sociologists, architects, and academicians are consulted and inputs from them are used while implementing the R&R program. A committee consisting of experts from the revenue department, engineering, forest, accounts and human resources department is formed for implementation of the R&R. In addition to monetary compensation and house plots for economic, physical, and socio-cultural rehabilitation, the farmers are compensated with other subsidiary compensation provisions. Those are described in Table 2-4.

Table 2-4: Provision of ex-gratia based on proportion of land acquired / submerged

Land holding lost (hectares)	Ex-gratia (Rs.)
0.25 to 3.50	60,000
3.51 to 6.75	40,000
6.76 to 10	20,000
> 10	Nil

Note: LPG is in addition to full compensation provided for acquired land.

Source: Adapted from GoK Report (2006).

For economic rehabilitation, subsidiary compensation provisions like a Land Purchase Grant (LPG), an Income Generating Scheme grant (IGS), waiver of stamp duty on purchase of land and house, vocational training and skill development programs, ex-gratia, and job reservation are made. In order to encourage repurchase of land after displacement, farmers are provided LPG depending up on the land holding lost due to acquisition (Table 2-4). The LPG is in addition to the compensation for land acquisition as per the LAA 1894.

For physical and socio-cultural rehabilitation, subsidiary compensation provisions like transportation facilities to newly allotted rehabilitation centers to carry the farmers' belongings, ex-gratia for construction of houses, and one time subsistence allowance along with initial groceries are provided. Monetary assistance or transportation facilities are provided to shift displaced families along with their livestock, housing, and farming materials and other belongings to newly allotted rehabilitation centers. The government assists the farmers to transport salvage materials of the old houses and structures to newly allotted rehabilitation centers, which can be used in construction of new houses. In addition to house plots and monetary compensation, each family is granted an ex-gratia of Rs. 22,000 for construction of house. One time subsistence allowance of Rs. 2800 along with free ration in the form of 40 Kgs of wheat, 40 Kgs of rice, 2 Kgs of sugar and 5 Liters of Kerosene is also provided in the first month of displacement (GoK, 2005).

2.4 Summary

This chapter gave an overall picture of institutional reforms of land acquisition and R&R of farmers in India, and the UKP in particular. It also highlighted the provisions and procedures followed in these process. Even after independence in 1947, the compensation component of the LAA 1894 was the only base for the R&R of displaced people. As the large developments projects mushroomed throughout India in order to meet the growing needs of increasing population and modernization, the R&R requirements of these projects started gaining importance. This is because of displacement of an increasing population and heightened public demand for effective R&R of such population. In pursuance of this, the government of India made gradual reforms in the R&R component of the LAA 1894. In addition, individual projects like the UKP modified these nationwide institutions of the R&R according to the situation and demand. Until recently there was no law as such for the R&R of displaced people in India. This institutional reform process and its insights serve as the bases of the empirical investigations of the thesis.

A key insight from this chapter is that the core principle of the contemporary institutional arrangement of the R&R is monetary compensation. It has been assumed that the monetary compensation principle is sufficient for efficient rehabilitation to be achieved. In the next chapter, the analytical framework to investigate the various questions analyzed throughout the thesis will be presented. The conceptual elements and the theoretical foundations of New Institutional Economics (NIE) required for institutional analysis of land acquisition and R&R of farmers will be explained.

Appendix

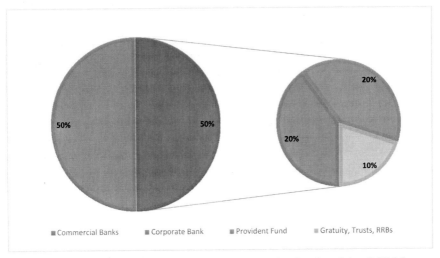

Figure 2-1: Share of major investors in the funds (bonds) of Krishna Bhagya Jala Nigam Ltd.

Source: Own compilation using the data from Gulati et al. (2005) and GoK (2014).

The KBJNL resulted from a successful institutional reform in reapproving the fund from the foreign funding sources (World Bank and Asian Development Bank) as well as in mobilizing the additional fund required to complete the UKP. This is mainly why the GoK formed the KBJNL as an autonomous body. Subsequently, for re-approval of funds suspended by the foreign funding sources due to lack of progress in the project implementation, the KBJNL triggered the pending works of the project to finish them within the stipulated time. Subsequently, the KBJNL succeeded in re-approval of some funds. While raising additional funds, the GoK transferred all the project assets to the KBJNL and made tripartite agreement between the GoK, the KBJNL, and the trustee[2] of bond holders. This is mainly to build investors' confidence in the KBJNL and to guarantee them their paybacks. The major investors are commercial banks, corporate banks, provident fund and gratuity, trusts and regional rural banks (RRBs) (Figure 2-1). Through this reform, the KBJNL gradually succeeded in raising funds and increased its share against share of the government in the total project expenditure. Until 1999, the KBJNL was successful in raising funds of about Rs.

---

[2] An authority on behalf of a company and bond holders / individual beneficiaries. In the UKP project, trustees are the different banks which acts an authority to manage bonds of the KBNL and bondholders.

11 billion, and its share in total expenditure raised from 29 per cent in 1995-96 to 98 per cent in 1998-99 (Figure 2-2 and Figure 2-3).

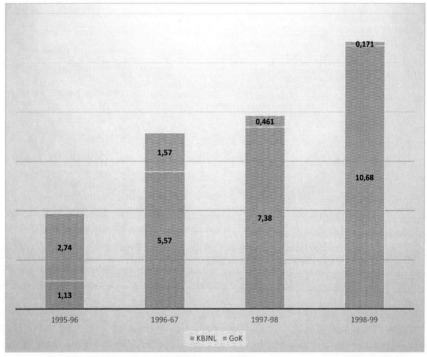

Figure 2-2: Share of Krishna Bhagya Jala Nigam Ltd. and government of Karnataka in Upper Krishna Project expenditure from 1995-96 to 1998-99 (Rs. Billion)

Source: Own compilation using the data from Gulati et al. (2005) and GoK (2014).

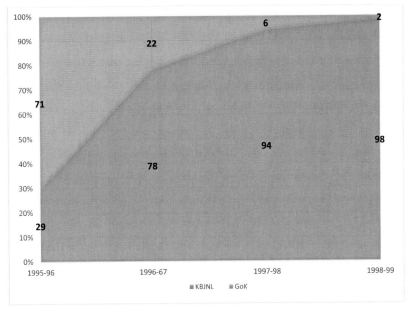

Figure 2-3: **Per cent Share of Krishna Bhagya Jala Nigam Ltd. and government of Karnataka in Upper Krishna Project expenditure from 1995-96 to 1998-99**

Source: Own compilation using the data from Gulati et al. (2005) and GoK (2014).

3 Theoretical Foundations

Overview

The reasoning behind Development-induced Displacement and Rehabilitation (DIDR) programs of land acquisition in India has a neoclassical orientation, focusing more on the monetary costs. However, rehabilitation of the displaced farmers is also influenced by institutions and governance structures. Therefore, in this chapter one such analytical framework, the institutions of sustainability (IoS), will be discussed which focuses on the properties of transactions and situates the dynamics of rehabilitation and resettlement (R&R) in an action arena. This provides the relevant foundations for the empirical analysis which ensues in the rest of the thesis.

3.1 Institutions of Sustainability: An Analytical Framework

The land acquisition issues and the associated compensation and R&R policies have been addressed by a cost-benefit approach that is based on strong assumptions of perfect information, complete rationality, and zero transaction costs. The discrepancies between these assumptions and the real action situation have often led to undesirable results in economic rehabilitation of farmers displaced due to development projects in India. This is reflected through its persistent symptoms of post-compensation marginalization and impoverishment of farmers. The approach misses the fact that rehabilitation of the farmers is not only influenced by those economic variables that are taken into account in a conventional cost-benefit approach but also by institutional arrangements and the modes of governance. As land is a prime input for agriculture, economic rehabilitation of displaced farmers is largely determined by land transactions post-displacement. This is reflected by economic variables such as compensation amounts, land prices and land availability. These variables in turn are predominantly driven by economic forces. For instance, as land prices usually rise post-compensation, this may cause difficulties for the farmers in finding land comparable in quantity and quality. In addition to these economic variables, rehabilitation of the farmers also depends on the way the government organizes and the efforts involved in it. Factors such as these need to be captured and, accordingly, a coherent analytical framework that encompasses these issues is needed to analyze post-displacement R&R problems of the farmers.

An analytical framework comprises a broad set of elements that are relevant to understand some real world phenomenon (McGinnis 2011). It identifies and categorizes such elements and their relationships, and in this way organizes the inquiry about institutions (McGinnis 2011; Ostrom 2011). Most of the frameworks in institutional analysis are intended to be general intellectual maps containing relevant elements which help in analyzing a wide range of social-ecological interactions (McGinnis 2011). Based on the nature of a particular problem, specific theories are used to generate and test important hypotheses. For conducting an appropriate institutional analysis of why the contemporary R&R program underperforms in economic rehabilitation of displaced farmers, this thesis uses the overarching analytical framework, the Institutions of Sustainability (*henceforth*, IoS) developed by Hagedorn (2008). The IoS framework is an analytical framework formulated for the analysis of institutions and governance structures that regularize co-evolutions of ecological and social systems. It provides an anatomy of institutional factors that helps to analyze and understand the complexity of determinants affecting an action situation. Taking 'transaction' as a unit of analysis, its general application lies in how institutions and governance structures develop or should develop for the purpose of regularizing nature-related transactions and resource management problems. The approach mainly assumes that institutions and governance structures that transform 'rules-in-form' into 'rules-in-use' emerge either spontaneously or deliberately in an action arena (Hagedorn 2008; Prager et al. 2011b).

However, the formation of particular institutions and governance structures that are able to achieve this transformation is determined by the properties of the respective transactions and the characteristics of involved actors (*ibid.*). This process takes place in action arenas where actors interact in an action situation (Hagedorn 2008). Therefore, the framework relates some key exogenous elements of institutional innovation and institutional performance and exhibits their significance in action arenas (as shown in the Figure 3-1). The elements are: institutions, governance structures, properties of transactions, and characteristics of actors (Hagedorn 2008; Prager et al. 2011b). They are interconnected and influence each other (Hagedorn 2008; Prager 2010). Action arenas comprise of an action situation and actors (Ostrom 2011). An action situation is "the social space where individuals interact, exchange goods and services, solve problems, dominate one another, or fight (among the many things that individuals do in action situations)" (*ibid.*).

Institutions are defined in a variety of ways although seemingly related. Ostrom (1990: 51) defines institutions as "the set of working rules that are used to determine who is eligible to make decisions in some arena, what actions are allowed or constrained, what aggregation rules will be used, what procedures must be followed, what information must or must not be provided, and what payoffs will be assigned to individuals dependent on their actions". North (1994) defines "institutions as formal rules, informal constraints (norms of behavior, conventions, and self-imposed codes of conduct) and the enforcement characteristics of both." Williamson (1996) uses the term institutional environment. For our purposes, institutions are defined as the set of formal and informal rules that regularize human actions and interactions. More specifically in the context of land acquisition, institutions are understood as formal rules that define procedures in the process of compensation.

Governance structures are the ways to organize transactions which are necessary in making institutions workable (Hagedorn 2008). Governance structures include markets, hierarchies, and hybrids (Williamson 1991; Ménard 2004; Hagedorn 2008). Hierarchies and markets are two ends on the conceptual spectrum of organizations. Hierarchy, on the one hand, is characterized by high administrative control in organizing transactions, where internalization of particular transactions takes place. There is unified or joint ownership that has high administrative control mechanisms and/or a centralized decision making system where top-down mechanisms work. On the other hand, the market mode is characterized by low administrative controls in organizing transactions. There is comparatively less mutual interdependency between transacting actors, who are usually large in number. The hybrid forms stand in between markets and hierarchies. Ménard (2004) calls them a "complex mix of strict hierarchy and broad decentralization".

By taking 'transaction' as the unit of analysis, the IoS framework facilitates institutional examination of economic activities related to natural resources. How to design adequate institutions and governance structures would depend on the properties of transactions. This is mainly because of the transaction-interdependence-institutions nexus (Hagedorn 2015). The properties of transactions cause particular forms of interdependence between actors. A transaction made by some actors not only affects them but also other actors, which creates interdependence (*ibid.*). Institutions and governance structures that regularize transactions are adequate if they fit to such interdependence. Asset specificity is one such property of a transaction. Asset specificity refers to the degree to which investments are necessary for durable transaction-specific assets (Williamson 1987b). The value of next best alternative use of such assets is significantly low which is because of their very low opportunity cost or salvage value. As asset specificity increases, bilateral dependency between actors intensifies and actors get locked into the transaction (Williamson 1981). In such a situation, hierarchy becomes the preferred mode of organizing transactions. When the asset is not very specific, market is a preferred mode of organizing transactions (Williamson 1985; Furubotn and Richter 2005). Williamson (1985, 1998) emphasizes different kinds of asset specificities – physical , human-capital, site and dedicated assets. Physical asset specificity arises when the physical property of an asset is very exclusive and makes it irrelevant outside a particular transaction. Human-capital specificity indicates specific human resources with specialized skills for a particular transaction. Site specificity arises when there are high costs of setup and/or relocation of an asset that is required for a particular transaction in some other place. Dedicated assets are those established by investments by a transacting party for the prospect of selling significant amount of a product to another particular transacting party (Joskow 1988). Uncertainty is another property of transactions that arises due to *ex-ante* and *ex-post* disturbances. Uncertainty can be categorized as behavioral uncertainty (strategic behavior / opportunism) and environmental (Williamson 1987a; Rindfleisch and Heide 1997). Environmental uncertainty arises due to lack of communication between actors, random natural events and technological uncertainty dealing with the difficulty to foresee and anticipate changes in the relevant environment (*ibid.*).

The design of institutions and governance structures also depend on the characteristics of actors associated with particular transactions. Institutions and governance structures regularize the conflicts or coordination between the actors. The characteristics of actors emphasized in the IoS framework are: attitudes, perceptions, information, knowledge, actors' method of action selection, values, beliefs, positions, reputation, trustworthiness, and political bargaining power of concerned actors (Gatzweiler and Hagedorn 2002). These characteristics serve as key variables in understanding decisions and expectations of concerned actors. Referring to the examples of agri-environmental problems like soil degradation, water scarcity, and agricultural land conversation, Gatzweiler and Hagedorn (2002) employ the IoS framework to analyze the role and importance of evolution of institutions for sustainable agri-environments. Prager (2010) uses several instances of agricultural soil degradation and conservation policies to operationalize the IoS framework. She unpacks the action arenas and analyzes the relationship between four exogenous variables – institutions, governance structures, physical properties of transactions, and characteristics of actors – and then links them to the actions situations. Prager et al. (2011a) compare two types of soil conservation policies – incentives-based policies and regulatory policy instruments (command and control). They find that policy effectiveness can be increased through precise technical measures coupled with enforcement mechanisms and recommend a mix of policies for tackling the different types of soil degradation.

Deneke et al. (2011), using the IoS framework, analyze two modes of governing local communal water and grazing resources – indigenous and externally initiated governance structures. They emphasize the institutional deficiencies and enforcement problems in communal water and grazing resources governance. It must be apparent to the reader now that the IoS framework focuses on the factors that determine institutional change and governance structures in an action situation. It analyses how institutions and governance structures change and perform to coordinate co-evolution of ecological and social systems (Gatzweiler and Hagedorn 2002). In addition, the IoS framework can also be applied to analyze and predict behavior of the actors within certain institutional arrangements, and evaluate their outcome. Verspecht et al. (2011) use this framework to assess the role of actor characteristics and awareness raising with regard to soil erosion, soil conservation practices and policies. This perspective provides policy insights which would have otherwise been ignored had a simpler neo-classical cost-benefit approach been the only analytical tool applied to the study of such problems. The next section lays down the key elements of the framework as applied to the context of R&R in involuntary land displacement. This narrative will bind the empirical analysis throughout the thesis into a coherent frame.

3.2 Decomposing the Framework for Empirical Analysis: An Outline

DIDR is the action arena in this study. Action situation is the involuntary acquisition of property from private owners for development projects, displacing them from their dwellings and livelihood sources, and rehabilitating them economically. Economic rehabilitation is a process of restoring farmers' standards of living.

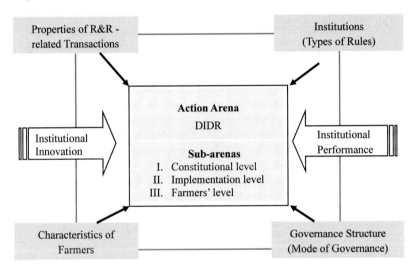

Figure 3-1: Adaptation of the Institutions of Sustainability (IoS) framework
Source: Adapted from Hagedorn (2008).

Figure 3-1 shows the four elements of the IoS framework that applies to the context of R&R: institutions, governance structures, properties of related transactions, and characteristics of farmers. Institutions of R&R indicate the formal rules to acquire land, displace farmers, and compensate them with monetary payments. These institutions comprise the rules to evaluate land for compensation, to notify farmers about the acquisition and the compensation, to allocate house plots and displace the farmers, and to claim the compensation. The detailed explanation of these institutions is provided in Sections 1.4 and 2.3. Governance structures of R&R indicate the modes of organizing rehabilitation processes. The contemporary and the newly drafted governance structures of R&R are discussed in detail in Sections 2.1 and 4.4.

The properties of R&R related transactions are post-displacement uncertainties involved in land repurchase, physical and locational specificity of land, and human capital specificity of displaced farmers. Chapter 4 discusses and analyzes these properties in a more detailed and constructed way. Characteristics of displaced farmers emphasize their resource holding, social identity, information about compensation claim methods, their decision making for the claim methods, and their expectations for R&R. These characteristics of farmers and their influence on outcome of R&R are analyzed in Chapters 5 and 6. The governance structures of R&R and the characteristics of displaced farmers are analyzed by decomposing the DIDR action situation.

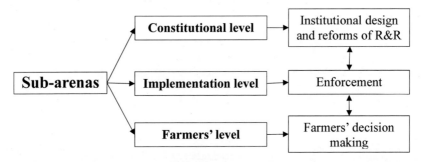

Figure 3-2: Decomposing action arena – development-induced displacement and rehabilitation

The actions relevant in the DIDR take place in three sub-arenas (Figure 3-2). The double arrow in Figure 3-2 represents the feedback from one to another. First is the constitutional level which contains the design of institutional arrangements of the R&R and mode of their organization. Second is the implementation level where these institutional arrangements and governance structures are implemented. Third is the stakeholder or the farmers' level in which is contained the farmer's decision in choosing particular compensation claim mechanism, reinvestment opportunities to them, and their preferences for compensation and/or rehabilitation provisions.

Using the lens of this multilevel framework, the thesis examines why the contemporary DIDR program is underperforming in economic rehabilitation of the farmers. This investigation facilitates in understanding whether institutions and governance structures for the DIDR have taken into consideration properties of transactions and characteristics of farmers, and its direct bearing on marginalization or rehabilitation of displaced farmers. To address this, the research question is decomposed into three sub-questions:

i.   How does the contemporary governance structure organize the DIDR and what are the implications? Using transaction cost reasoning, the analysis focuses on properties of the DIDR-related transactions, current institutions and governance structures, and action situations in the implementation level sub-arena and its link to the constitutional level sub-arena.

ii. What are the institutional arrangements of the R&R and its implications on farmers' decision to claim compensation? The analysis of this question focuses on characteristics of the farmers, current institutional arrangements, and action situations in the implementation and farmer's level sub-arena.

iii. What are the farmers' preferences towards the DIDR provisions? This question examines whether there is a mismatch between the preferences and the provisions of the contemporary DIDR program. This is primarily situated in the farmer's level sub-arena although is inclusive of key insights from the other sub-arenas.

The combined results would provide a better understanding of why displaced farmers get further marginalized. However, this is possible only when linked with appropriate theories. The empirical chapters are, therefore, based on rigorous and specific theoretical perspectives. Chapter 4 is founded on a detailed explanation of transaction cost economics. One way to analyze the contemporary governance structure for organizing the DIDR is comparing the costs of organizing these transactions with those of other alternative structures. In this approach, the governance structure that minimizes transaction costs vis-a-vis other alternative structures is considered to be efficient. Another way is comparing its actual outcome with the intended outcome. In this approach, if the actual outcome is equal to or more than the intended outcome then that particular governance structure is considered to be efficient. Hence, using transaction cost theory, a comparative analysis of the contemporary governance structure and the newly proposed mode of organizing the DIDR is done to address the first research sub-question - how the contemporary governance structure organizes the DIDR and what the implications are.

A right is always accompanied by rules that specify choices a right-holder may, must or must not make in order to exercise it. The displaced farmers' decision to claim compensation depends on their characteristics and on the availability of choices provided by the contemporary institutional arrangements. As detailed in Chapter 2, the right to claim compensation of land acquisition is specified by rules which specify two methods of claim – the consent method and the general method. It is observed that the majority of displaced farmers in most cases claimed their compensation through consent award in spite of having an incentive to claim higher compensation through the General Award (GA). This observation, therefore, posits a question: what factors influence this choice? Moreover, their choices raise a doubt: whether the allocated property rights to claim compensation are sufficient to achieve the intended benefits. Theorizing *access*-based property rights distribution explains the factors that influence the choice of the farmers. This is elaborated in Chapter 5. The variables derived from this theory facilitate in analyzing the second sub-research question - what are the institutional arrangements of the DIDR and its implications on farmers' decision to claim compensation?

As emphasized by Young (2002), "to be effective, institutional arrangements need to be well-matched to the defining features of the problems they address." Therefore, institutional arrangements of the DIDR need to be matched with local situations and farmers' expectations. Using the concept of fit, this is tested in the third sub-research question - what are the farmers' preferences towards the DIDR provisions? This analysis of farmers' preferences could stimulate further discussions on how institutions change. The concept of institutional fit is detailed in the Chapter 6. Taking the IoS framework as a starting point, these three different yet related approaches are adopted to diagnose the R&R problem and then provide unique perspectives which would eventually allow the framing of more appropriate and fit institutions.

3.3 Summary

The DIDR programs of land acquisition in most of the developing countries reflect the reasoning of a largely neoclassical approach, where only economic variables are taken into account. However, rehabilitation of the displaced farmers is also influenced by institutions and governance structures. Hence, a coherent analytical framework for such an analysis is needed for conducting appropriate research on the post-displacement rehabilitation and resettlement (R&R) problems of the affected farmers. Hence, a coherent analytical framework that encompasses such institutional aspects is needed for institutional analysis of the post-displacement R&R problems of the farmers. An overarching analytical framework developed by Hagedorn (2008) – the Institutions of Sustainability (IoS) framework - fulfills this requirement. Theories are used to focus on specific elements of the framework, which are relevant to address associated research question(s) by formulating hypothesis based on the variables selected from those theories. The IoS framework comprises four main elements of institutional analysis – institutions, governance structures, characteristics of actors and properties of transactions. The question of why the contemporary DIDR program fails to achieve intended outcomes then calls for an empirical investigation of the contemporary governance structure and institutional arrangements of the DIDR from the farmers' perspective. In order to address this question, first a comparative analysis of governance structures is conducted using transaction cost theory. Secondly, by using the access-based property rights approach, the thesis investigates contemporary institutional arrangements of the DIDR and its implications for farmers' decision to claim compensation. Finally, as farmers' characteristics and their expectations play an important role in the rehabilitation process, the concept of fit is used to analyze the farmers' preferences towards the DIDR provisions. Taking the IoS framework as a starting point, these three different yet related approaches are adopted to unpack the rehabilitation problems.

4 Transaction Costs and Farmer Marginalization in Land Acquisition[1]

Overview

In developing countries, the general principle followed in land acquisition for infrastructure projects is monetary compensation, which amounts to multiple times the registered value of land. The idea is to minimize deviation from market prices so that farmers can buy comparable land assets. Despite this monetary compensation, a large proportion of the farming population ends up not owning comparable assets and thus gets further marginalized. Therefore, in recent times there have been attempts to reform the rehabilitation mechanism. In this chapter, the problem of marginalization is explained using a transaction cost analysis of the dominant land acquisition framework in India (LAA 1894). Based on the case of displaced farmers of the Upper Krishna project in Karnataka, we show how specificities related to land characteristics, uncertainties in search for alternatives and information constraints impose high non-monetary transaction costs on farmers. We then assess whether or not the newly proposed land acquisition framework (RFCTLARR 2015) promises to lower transaction costs on farmers.

4.1 Introduction

After independence from the colonial regime in 1947, several large dam projects have been implemented in India. India stands third among the countries having most dams in the world, with more than 5000 large dams (GoI 2009). The objectives of these projects have been irrigation supply along with hydropower generation and flood control. But in this process, a large population has been affected due to involuntary appropriation of land and displaced nearly 60 million people in India since independence (Choudhury 2013). Cernea (2004) lists the effects of displacement as loss of land, homes, jobs, marginalization, food insecurity and community disarticulation. In the absence of effective resettlement, these are the negative impacts of involuntary transactions[2] imposed on farmers due to development projects. The efforts displaced farmers need to make in order to regain their income and standard of living are transaction costs imposed on them. Institutional arrangements for the rehabilitation and resettlement (R&R) of displaced

---

[1]   This chapter is presented at the 53th Annual Conference of the German Society of Economic and Social Sciences in Agriculture, 25.-27.09.2013, Berlin, Germany. It is also selected for poster presentation in 29th Triennial Conference of the International Association of Agricultural Economists (IAAE), August 08 – 14, 2015, Milan, Italy.
[2]   Involuntary Transaction is a transaction that one participant does not wish to enter into, but is required to by some external force or dominant agent or regulations and laws (Pammachius 2011).

people are designed by governments to minimize such transaction costs, given the constraints of limited post-displacement opportunities, and capabilities and skills of farmers.

However, organization of the R&R procedure is a very complex process and is generally given low importance in project implementation (Cernea 1997). Mainly there are three disruptions from involuntary transactions of farmers' land and houses – social, physical, and economic. Hence, in order to minimize impacts of disruption, rehabilitation of all the three types of disruptions needs to be considered by project authorities (Jaamdar 2006). Physical rehabilitation implies restoring houses and basic infrastructure facilities like water, electricity, road, public transport. Socio-cultural rehabilitation implies restoring social capital, relations, or networks, and keeping culture and beliefs intact. Economic rehabilitation implies restoring peoples' income at least to their previous level.

In India, the Land Acquisition Act (LAA) 1894 provides the broad framework for land acquisition and farmers' rehabilitation. The general principle followed for acquisition of land and other immoveable assets of farmers for infrastructure projects like irrigation is *monetary compensation*. It is implicitly assumed that monetary compensation achieves economic rehabilitation[3] and restores the original standard of living. In order to minimize the deviation from the market prices and so as to enable the farmer's ability to purchase comparable land assets, the value of monetary compensation is multiple times the registered value of the land. Yet, large proportions of them end up owning far less assets and thus get further marginalized (Cernea 1997, 2003; Kanbur 2003; Mathur 2006a).

In this paper, we apply a transaction cost framework to explain why such a deviation takes place using the case of the Upper Krishna Irrigation Project (UKP) in the northern part of Karnataka, India. We show how specificities related to land characteristics, uncertainties in search for alternatives, and information constrains impose high non-monetary transaction costs on farmers. We use the same analytical framework to make a preliminary assessment of the new draft legislation called the Right to Fair Compensation and Transparency in Land Acquisition, Rehabilitation and Resettlement (RFCTLARR) (Amendment) Ordinance 2015, which replaces the older legislation. We try to gauge whether the new legislation reduces the burdens of transaction costs on farmers.

The remainder of the chapter has five sections: Section 4.2 describes the problem of rehabilitation in Upper Krishna Project. Section 4.3 discusses theoretical foundations of transaction cost approach and reviews related literature. This approach facilitates us to hypothesize that there are the high transaction costs that farmers incurred, which led to their failure to regain their income post-displacement and marginalization. Complexities of land purchase transactions and rehabilitation is analyzed in Section 4.4, which presents the *ex-*

---

[3] As we restricted this study to only economic rehabilitation, use of the term 'rehabilitation' in remaining parts of the article represents only economic rehabilitation.

post transaction costs incurred by the farmers. The comparative transaction cost analysis of the new and proposed R&R is presented in Section 4.5. Finally, Section 4.6 provides the conclusions and scope for further research.

4.2 The Problem of Rehabilitation in Upper Krishna Project

The river Krishna is an inter-state river passing through one Western and two Southern states of India namely Maharashtra, Karnataka, and Andhra Pradesh. The river inflow is very high during the monsoon and low during the summer. In order to regulate the wide fluctuation of the river flow and provide irrigation throughout the year, the Government of Karnataka proposed an irrigation project called the UKP in the year 1963. The objectives of the project were to provide irrigation to the drought prone rainfed areas, to increase agricultural production, farmers' income, and employment as well as to generate electric power. The project covers the districts of: Bagalkot, Bijapur, Raichur and Gulbarga (GoI 2010). Two dams have been already built in the region: Almatti and Narayanpur dams. In total, 833,600 hectares of agricultural land is estimated to be irrigated under the UKP providing a Full Reservoir Level (FRL) of approximately 524 meters (*ibid.*). Upon completion, the project also generates power of about 150 megawatt (MW). However, even as the UKP provided irrigation to a large area and thus benefited the farmers living in the *command area*, it has also displaced a large number of farmers, nearly a population of 487,576 and 201 villages in the *catchment area* (*ibid.*).

Table 4-1: Stages of Upper Krishna Project with village and population displacement

Sl. No	Stage	Dam	Implementation period	No. of villages affected	Population displaced	Land acquisition (Hectare)
1	Stage I	Narayanpur and Almatti	1982-1997	138 (+54)	320,000	38,668
2	Stage II	Almatti	1997-2000	42 (+1)	80,000	66,338
3	Stage III	Almatti	Yet to be displaced	22	87,576	45,875
	Total			**202 (+55)**	**487,576**	**150,881**

Note: Figures in the parenthesis indicate the partly submerged villages.

Source: Own compilation from various government reports (GoK 2006, 2012, 2013a).

As can be seen in Table 4-1, in the first two stages of the three stage project, 179 villages and a city have been submerged and 400,000 people have been displaced. The third stage of the project is still under implementation and is set to submerge 22 villages displacing a population of 87,576 villagers.

The affected villagers are provided monetary and non-monetary compensation based on the evaluations of experts and as per the land acquisition rules of the government (see Table 4-5 in Section 4.4). However, the standard of living and social status of most of the people have deteriorated after their displacement (GoK 2004). This resulted in several small and marginal farmers becoming landless labors. Parasuraman (1996) analyzes the cases of the UKP stage I and finds that medium farmers became small and small farmers went below poverty line after displacement. Many of the landless farmers migrated to nearby big cities for construction work. World Bank (1998) evaluated involuntary resettlement impact of the Upper Krishna projects of Karnataka and Maharashtra and found that 80-90 per cent of the displaced people were not able to purchase comparable land at all and those who could, either purchased lesser quantum or poorer quality land. This shows that although the farmers have been offered monetary compensation for their lost land and houses (under the R&R program of the LAA 1894) the problems of rehabilitation remain.

This is despite the fact that the compensation design of the R&R is flexible and takes two forms: the 'consent award' (CA) and the 'general award' (GA). Based on a three year average registered and prevailing market value of the land in the vicinity, an evaluation committee fixes the land value. In the CA, farmers receive a compensation amount that is multiple times (to bring it as close as possible to market price) the fixed value of land. In return, farmers have to sign a consent agreement that they would not approach the court for claiming further compensation. In case the farmers find the compensation amount of the CA inadequate, they can reject the CA and opt for the GA. In the GA, farmers initially get the compensation just equal to the registered value and are allowed to claim higher compensation through litigation. However, the litigations could run up to several years and the amount is dependent on the cropping pattern followed by a particular farmer.[4]

Since secondary data is not adequately available on the figures of the population choosing between the CA and the GA, we conducted 200 farmer interviews in the year 2013 in eight randomly selected villages that are displaced in the UKP (Figure 4-1). Information was collected on farmers' pre- and post-displacement socioeconomic status. Questions about their choice of the award in claiming the monetary compensation and problems faced in that process were asked. Interviews were also conducted with 25 government officials and questions on the organizational processes and issues of land acquisition, apportion-

---

[4] Major cropping pattern in the submerged area is seasonal crops like Maize, Cotton, Onion, Wheat, and vegetables; annual crops like Sugarcane; and perennial crops like Grapes, Lemon, Pomegranate, Sapota, etc. Valuation of land with perennial crops also includes valuation of plantations and associated structures like fence, drip irrigation, supporting structures, etc. Hence land valuation is usually higher in case of plantation crops.

ment methods of monetary compensation, provisions of rehabilitation policy and their impact of displaced farmers were included.

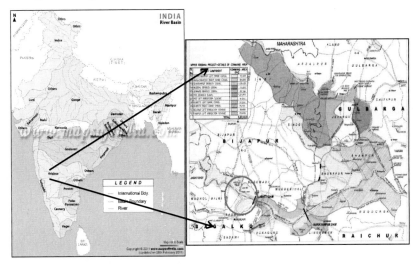

Figure 4-1: Enlarged view of Upper Krishna Project index map
Source: Modified using the maps taken from (MoI 2012; GoI 2014)

As shown in Table 4-2, 55 per cent of the interviewed farmers chose the CA, while 45 per cent opted for the GA. It took a minimum of six and maximum of 36 months to claim the compensation through the CA (with an average of 11 months). For the GA, it took a minimum of 24 and maximum of 180 months (with an average of 36 months) to receive compensation[5]. In the rest of the paper, we argue that an important reason for farmers getting worse-off in spite of a flexible compensation mechanism is the high *ex-post* transaction costs imposed on them due to a faulty governance structure of compensation.

---

[5] The figures for the GA are not exact as some of the litigations have not yet been resolved.

Table 4-2: Farmers' scenario after displacement

Sl. No	Particulars	CA			GA			t test
		Marginal & small holdings	Medium & large	Total	Marginal & small holdings	Medium & large	Total	
1	Percent of total sample	41	14	55	34	11	45	
2	Farmers not purchased land (%)	44	8	52	37	11	48	
3	Farmers purchased land (%)	33	29	62	25	13	38	
4	Farmers purchased land less than they lost (%)	32	36	68	12	20	32	
5	Illiterate (%)	50	8	58	32	10	42	
6	Less educated (up to 10th standard) (%)	41	12	53	34	13	47	
7	Farmers whose income decreased (%)	43	11	54	35	11	46	
8	Minimum time taken to claim (months)		6			24		
9	Maximum time taken to claim (months)		36			180[#]		
10	Average time taken to claim (months)		11			40		0.00***

Notes: # The figures indicate only those who received the compensation amount so far. There are a few farmers who are in the middle of pursuing litigation; Marginal & smallholdings refer to less those having than 2ha, and medium and large refer to 2ha and above

Source: Author's own compilation and (Misri 2006)

4.3   A Transaction Cost Perspective: Theoretical Foundations

The literature examining marginalization of people displaced due to development projects largely focuses on the compensation principle. There is evidence showing that compensation is underestimated and that resettlement policies are compensation-centered and not income-centered (Cernea 2004; Mathur 2006c). Cernea (2003) shows that displaced farmers misdirected their compensation to non-income generating activities. Moreover, the value of assets appreciate after the determination and distribution of compensation, due to which farmers' purchasing power diminishes. De Wet (2006b) ascribes the main cause of marginalization to a lack of national legal frameworks and policies, commitment to implement, funding, planning, consultation, and enforcement. Post-displacement loss of social capital is yet another cause (Kanbur 2003).

In addition to direct compensation mechanisms and its variants, other policy measures are needed to tackle the problems of displacement   (Cernea 2003; Kanbur 2003). Kanbur (2003) proposes "generalized safety nets" as a complement to the project specific compensation mechanisms in order to achieve equitable benefits. Cernea (2003) prescribes "development-oriented investment," along with compensation to ensure sustainable income generation of displaced people. In India, compensation for land is based on historical registered value, which neglects the subjective value of landowner and subsequently results in under-compensation. This is important as the subjective value is a part of the opportunity cost of land acquisition (Lueck and Miceli 2004).

Several studies on land acquisition focus on the link between compensation and investment decisions of landowners before actual land acquisition and displacement (*ibid.*). However, rarely do studies focus on the link between the compensation and land owners' *post-displacement* investment decisions to restore their income. This is critical as farmers in India usually have very low levels of literacy and hence have little skills other than agriculture and allied activities. The prime input for agriculture is land. Being engaged in irrigated agriculture before displacement, most of the farmers prefer to continue in agriculture, which however, requires land. The projects base their efficiency criteria on cost-benefit analysis and ignore post-displacement organizational domain of the R&R. This is despite the fact that there is growing awareness among the scholars, as discussed above, and policy makers that the monetary compensation principle of land acquisition fails to regain income of displaced people. We therefore bring in a discussion of transaction cost economics (TCE) which helps understand how the post-displacement situation could be an important departure from realization of efficient rehabilitation.

TCE applies to the study of different kinds of economic organization of transactions (Williamson 1985). Development projects involve involuntary transactions like the acquisition of land and houses. TCE addresses the problem of organizing transactions, by comparative analysis of different governance structures employed in the transaction of a good or service. According to Williamson (1985) "a transaction occurs when a good or service is transferred across a technologically separable interface. One stage of activity terminates and another begins" (p.1). Which mode of governance structure should be preferred for organizing a transaction, depends on the characteristics of the transaction and the transaction cost incurred in the respective mode (Williamson 1987b, 1998). There are three distinct generic modes of governance (Williamson 1991): markets, hybrids and hierarchies. Williamson (1991) differentiates these three modes of governance based on contract law, adaptability to consequential disturbances, administrative control, and use of incentives (Table 4-3).

Table 4-3: Distinguishing attributes of leading generic modes of governance

Governance attributes	Governance modes		
	Market	**Hybrid**	**Hierarchy**
Incentives	High-powered	Medium-powered	Low-powered
Administrative support by bureaucracy	Nil	Some	Much
Contract law regime	Legalistic	Contract as framework	Firm as own court of ultimate appeal (Fiat)

Source: Williamson (2003)

In the market form, transactions are laterally integrated between known (or unknown) actors in a fairly impersonal setting (Williamson 1991). For example, farmer water markets involving buying and selling of bore well water. Actors act autonomously and make their own decisions while adapting to disturbances, as they are not relied on administrative controls. A farmer decides from whom to buy water and if there are any changes in the expected prices, and quality or quantity, he accordingly adapts and buy from other sellers. Hence, there is no bilateral dependency between the actors in market as there is high incentive intensity.

In a hierarchical mode of governance, transactions are vertically integrated, and highly administratively controlled with bureaucratic costs (Williamson 1991). For example, a way of organizing irrigation water by a farmer through drilling a borewell on his own farm, instead of buying of water from others through some arrangements. Intended cooperation between the actors needs to be high while adapting to the disturbances in organizing transactions through hierarchy. Hence, there is a strong bilateral dependency and low incentive intensity.

The hybrid mode lies in between market and hierarchy forms in terms of contract law, adaptability, administrative control, and use of incentives. For example, a farmer drills a borewell on another farmer's farm and makes a long-term contract for the provision of irrigation water with safeguards against *ex-post* uncertainties. Actors enjoy some autonomy, which encourages acting efficiently without consulting the other. Hence, the hybrid form is featured with an intermediate degree of administrative control and semi-legalistic contract law regime, and semi-strong adaptations and incentives (Williamson 1991). Depending on attributes of the transaction and their differential costs (Ménard 2004), a transaction is best organized under one of these three governance structures. The main principle here is based on the efficiency criteria for managing transactions through alternative governance structures. That is, discriminating alignment hypothesis – economizing based on transaction costs (Williamson 2005). Complex transactions involve (transaction) costs due to their particular attributes. Hence, a system that minimizes the transaction costs is more efficient in allocating the property rights (Lueck and Miceli 2004).

In conventional Transaction Cost Economic, the three important attributes of transaction are: asset specificity, uncertainty, and frequency (Williamson 1981). Asset specificity refers to the degree to which the investments are necessary for durable, transaction-specific assets (Williamson 1987b). The value of next best alternative use of such assets is significantly low. This attribute creates a condition of bilateral dependency. The dependency between the actors intensifies as asset specificity deepens and actors locked into the transaction (Williamson 1981). Therefore, both the parties have to make special efforts to protect investments and continue cooperation either by implementing, monitoring, and enforcing contractual safeguards through credible commitments (Williamson 1987b; Rindfleisch and Heide 1997) or by way of unified ownership (hierarchy) (Williamson 1987b). As Williamson (1998) emphasizes, asset specificity can be physical asset specificity, human-capital specificity, site specificity, dedicated asset specificity, brand name capital, and temporal specificity. For economic rehabilitation under contemporary framework, physical asset specificity (land), site, or location specificity (nearby their location) and human capital specificity (agricultural skills) are common forms.

The main distinguishing assumption of transaction cost theory is bounded rationality. That is, transacting actors have incomplete information and limited mental capacity, because of which they incur high transaction costs due to uncertainty they face about unforeseen events and outcomes (Shirley and Ménard 2005). Uncertainty is considered broadly under two sources, environmental variability and behavioral uncertainty (Rindfleisch and Heide 1997). Environmental uncertainties are of unintentional kind, such as uncertainty due to lack of communication between actors, uncertainty due to random natural acts and technological uncertainty dealing with the difficulty to foresee and anticipate changes in the relevant environment (Rindfleisch and Heide 1997). Williamson (1987a) considers strategic behavior (opportunism) as a behavioral uncertainty. To safeguard against unforeseen environmental uncertainties, making complete contracts is difficult for which renegotiation and adaption is required (Williamson 1979). With this theoretical understanding, we analyze the complexities involved in post-displacement transactions of rehabilitation under the contemporary mode of governance.

4.4 Complexities of Land Purchase Transactions and Rehabilitation

The objective behind the monetary compensation mechanism is to minimize the deviation from the market prices so that farmers can buy comparable land assets. The rehabilitation process involves two interconnected sub-transactions - apportionment of monetary compensation by the government to displaced farmers and purchase of comparable land assets by the displaced farmers from other land sellers. This resembles a hybrid governance structure, when viewed from the transaction cost perspective (Figure 4-2), where there is an 'administrative support by bureaucracy' in provision of monetary compensation but then leaves the farmers in an open land market where only medium-powered incentives are available. Figure 4-2 shows that with funding and institutional assistance of Government of India and international funding agencies like the World Bank and the Asian Development Bank, the Government of Karnataka currently governs land acquisition and rehabilitation of affected people. The Land Acquisition officers and the R&R officers jointly conduct land valuation, land acquisition, apportionment of monetary compensation, and other rehabilitation processes. Until here, the process is governed in a hierarchical form. After this, farmers are autonomous decision makers to allocate their compensation amount for their future income generation. However, as lack of education and skills could create a lock-in situation for farmers to move out of agriculture, it is inevitable for them to purchase land in order to generate income through agriculture. Therefore, farmers have to organize land transactions in land market by themselves (Figure 4-2).

However, rehabilitation of affected people as a whole is a very complex transaction, which creates interconnectedness among different actors like government, displaced farmers, and land sellers in the land market. The complexity is mainly because of interconnected sub-transactions, the attributes of rehabilitation, and characteristics of actors involved in the action situation. Under apportionment of compensation, there are complexities involved in the valuation of submerged land, compensation amount to be provided, and *ex-post* inflation of land price. Purchase of land is also a complex transaction because of the distorted land market in India.

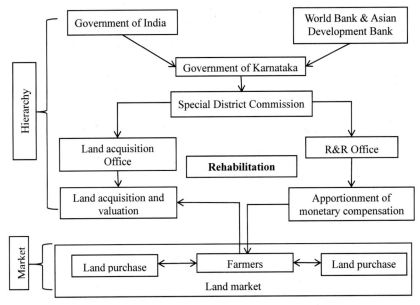

Figure 4-2: Contemporary framework of rehabilitation

Note: Arrow indicates the transaction

Source: Author's own compilation

Farmers have less information, knowledge, and predictive capacity about the post-displacement outcomes as well as land availability, quality, location, and inflation of land price in the vicinity. Hence, the rehabilitation agreement between the farmers and the government is incomplete. In addition, during interviews many farmers expressed the strategic behavior of the land sellers based on the information about the compensation amount they got and high demand for land in the vicinity. These explanations are evident in our study area. Among the total number of farmers interviewed, 25 per cent of farmers are illiterates and 75 per cent of the farmers are educated less than the high school (<10th standard) (see Table 4-2). The survey also shows that 74 per cent of the displaced farmers could not purchase any land using the compensation amount. Among 26 per cent of those farmers who could purchase land, 48 per cent purchased land less than their original holding. In addition, for 85 per cent of the farmers their net income reduced. Among these, 53 per cent are those who opted for the CA and 47 per cent who opted the GA. These investigations clearly show that the farmers are marginalized as compared to pre-displacement scenario.

Table 4-4: Attributes of land purchase for sampled farmers

Attributes	Details	Sample scenario
Location	Average distance from newly purchased land to allotted dwelling place (Kilometer)	20
Type of land	Percentage of farmers purchasing dry land	61
	Percentage of farmers purchasing irrigated land	39
Land quality	Among the farmers who purchased land, those got worse quality of land than previously owned	50
	Same quality land than previously owned	39
	Better quality land than previously owned	11
Time	Average time taken to purchase land (years)	3.7
Information	Farmers having no information about compensation claiming methods *ex-ante* (%)	74
	Farmers having information about compensation claiming methods *ex-ante* (%)	26
Compensation utilization	Farmers who spent their compensation amount on non-income generating activities either fully or partially (%)	66
	On an Average, percent of compensation amount spent of non-income generating activities	61

Source: Own compilation using survey data

Table 4-4 shows attributes of farmers' land transactions post-displacement. An average distance from the allotted dwelling place to newly purchased land is 20 kilometer (km), which means there is uncertainty of getting land even if farmers go up to 20 km. Although farmers go up to or beyond 20 km, there is uncertainty of getting similar quality of land as they had earlier. Among the farmers who purchased land, 61 per cent purchased dry land, whereas they had irrigated land earlier. More than 50 per cent of the farmers purchased poor quality land in terms of fertility, irrigation, and other characteristics. From these dry and poor quality land, farmers realize less income than before. In addition, farmers were uncertain about the time needed to search and buy the land. On an average, the farmers took 3 years and 8 months to purchase land after they received their compensation amount. This temporal gap in purchasing the land is one of the main reasons that widen the gap between compensation amount and price of land per acre. These uncertainties yield high *ex-post* transaction costs on farmers making them incapable to purchase land for their future income generation. Even if they purchased, they could purchase less than what they had forgone in the acquisition process. Among the sample farmers who purchased land, 48 per cent purchased lesser than that they lost (see Table 4-2). Even if the farmers purchased the same or larger sized land than what they have forgone, either that land was dryland or poor quality land (as mentioned above). Majority of the farmers (66 per cent) invested their compensation either fully or partially on non-income generating activities like marriages, repayment of previous loans, house construction, and alcoholism among others. This reflects farmers' lack of portfolio management skills in utilizing their compensation amount.

TCE presents an option of internalizing a transaction in the absence of credible commitment through safeguards for post-contractual hazards. Since the Government of India has recently drafted a new form[1] of organizing economic rehabilitation, we compare it with the present mode and try to analyze whether provisions of the new legislation address the *ex-post* transactions costs incurred by the farmers. Table 4-5 shows the main differences in the newly drafted legislation called the Right to Fair Compensation and Transparency in Land Acquisition, Rehabilitation and Resettlement (amendment) ordinance (RFCTLARR 2015)[2].

In the new legislation, the government internalizes some part of open market land purchase and provides 'land for land' compensation instead. The rest will continue to be made through cash compensation. Cash compensation for remaining land has been increased few folds in the new ordinance, that is, two times the market value of land in urban areas and four times the market value in

---

[1] The new law was passed in 2013 but ever since there was a change in government which brought new amendments and hence the change is still in progress.

[2] The basic prescription of the ordinance is as follows: "An Act to ensure, in consultation with institutions of local self-government and Gram Sabhas established under the Constitution, a humane, participative, informed and transparent process for land acquisition for industrialization, development of essential infrastructural facilities and urbanization with the least disturbance to the owners of the land and other affected families and provide just and fair compensation to the affected families whose land has been acquired or proposed to be acquired or are affected by such acquisition and make adequate provisions for such affected persons for their rehabilitation and resettlement and for ensuring that the cumulative outcome of compulsory acquisition should be that affected persons become partners in development leading to an improvement in their post-acquisition social and economic status and for matters connected therewith or incidental thereto" (for more details see the RFCTLARR (Amendment) Ordinance 2015 and its previous versions).

rural areas. Farmers will also be provided minimum land by the displacing agency itself in case of irrigation projects. In addition, a provision for guaranteed job has been introduced, where one person in each family gets a job in either the private or government sectors. This aims to address concerns of farmers and those whose livelihoods are dependent on the land being acquired, while at the same time facilitating land acquisition for industrialization, infrastructure and urbanization projects in a timely and transparent manner.

Table 4-5: Provisions of current and new rehabilitation and resettlement frameworks

Sl. No.	Provisions	Current rehabilitation framework	New framework
1	Monetary compensation	Fixed based on the evaluation committee	Four times the market value of the land in rural area and two times in urban
2	Land for land lost in irrigation projects	No	At least one acre land should be provided in command area of the Irrigation project
3	Job provision clause	5% job reservation in government departments	Compulsory provision of job to one person in each affected family
4	Solatium	15-30% of total compensation amount	100% of total compensation
5	Farmers' consent for acquisition	No	Consent of 70 to 80% of land owners in private based projects
6	Information provision	Yes	Yes
7	Preparation and appraisal of SIA study by an expert group	No	Yes

Note: Current rehabilitation framework is the LAA 1894 and its amendments and new framework is the RFCT-LARR (amendment) ordinance 2015.

Source: Adopted from the government reports and RFCTLARR (Amendment) Ordinance, 2015

4.5 Comparative Transaction Cost Analysis of New and Proposed Rehabilitation and Resettlement

Table 4-6 presents a comparative view of the important sources of transaction costs for farmers in the current and newly proposed frameworks. The first and second attributes refer to the human capital specificity and the physical specificity of land that is prime input for the farmers to regain their income. This is mainly because farmers have low education levels (see Table 4-2) and have limited income generating skills other than agriculture. This limits the income generating opportunities farmers have outside agriculture. Hence, farmers are skilled specific to agriculture, and land is a physical asset highly specific for the farmers' future income generation in the current mode of rehabilitation (Table 4-6). Whereas, in case of new mode of organizing rehabilitation, there are provisions of 1-2.5 acres of land in irrigation projects and a compulsory job to one person in each family. These clauses in the new mode make the land comparatively less physical asset specific.

Table 4-6: Transaction characteristics in existing and proposed rehabilitation and resettlement

Sl. No.	Attributes of transaction	Current mode	New mode
1	Human capital specificity (Farmers' skill limited to Agriculture)	High	High
2	Physical asset specificity (Land)	High	(Comparatively) Low
3	Locational asset specificity (Location of Land)	High	Low
4	Information (Information about the compensation claiming methods)	Low	High
5	Uncertainty A (Location of land to be purchased)	High	Low
6	Uncertainty B (Uncertainty of land price)	High	Low
7	Uncertainty C (Availability of comparable land (size))	High	Low
8	Uncertainty D (Uncertainty about water availability and other quality parameters of land)	High	Low
9	Uncertainty E (Time to search and buy land)	High	Low

Source: Compiled from field work observations and review of reports of current and new rehabilitation provisions.

The third attribute refers to locational specificity of land. Farmers are allocated house plots for their physical rehabilitation in the current mode and they have to purchase land by themselves in the current mode of organizing rehabilitation. Farmers look for land preferably not far from the allocated house plot. Land in the vicinity becomes high locational specific asset for the farmers to rehabilitate economically. This high locational asset specificity increases the demand of land in the surrounding areas. As mentioned in Section 4.4, the land sellers behave strategically as a result of this high demand and based on the compensation announcement of land. Hence, there is an uncertainty about the location of land and its distance from their dwelling place, and price of land (Uncertainty A and B). Whereas in case of new mode, as land for land and house site is allocated in the benefited area of the irrigation project, land is less location asset specific for the farmers. Since government itself allots land, farmers will not face uncertainty of land price.

As mentioned in Section 4.4, farmers have incomplete information about land markets and bounded rationality to deal with land transactions (lack of information). In addition, majority of the farmers have marginal and small land holdings (75 per cent in the study sample (see Table 4-2)), searching similar sized land takes some more time and cost. As a result, they faced high uncertainty in getting comparable land of their preferred size (Uncertainty C). Among those who purchased land, the majority of them (more than 50 per cent) purchased dry and worse land. This shows the uncertainty of getting irrigated and better quality land (Uncertainty D).

As a results of these specificities and uncertainties, there are high uncertainties in terms of time required to search and purchase land (Uncertainty E), where they may or may not get land immediately. Even if farmers are able to buy the land, they are uncertain about irrigation water availability, soil type, and soil fertility as compared to their submerged land. Under new the R&R framework, the government takes up the responsibility to allocate land in the benefited areas, thereby reducing uncertainties for the farmers.

Even though the new legislation intends to address the *ex-post* transactions costs through internalizing land transactions enforcement will remain an important challenge. However, a discussion of that is beyond the scope of this paper.

4.6   Conclusion

Development-induced displacement imposes involuntary transactions on farmers. These transactions, especially in developing countries, are very complex and interconnected, which cause social, physical, and economic disruptions to farmers. But in this process, a large population has been affected due to involuntary appropriation of land and displaced nearly 60 million people in India since independence (Choudhury 2013). The general principle followed for land acquisition is *monetary compensation,* which, from a cost-benefit approach, is assumed to be sufficient for rehabilitation of farmers. However, it has failed to realize the desired outcome of rehabilitation, and large proportions of displaced farmers end up owning far less assets and thus get further marginalized. Therefore, we enquire why the present approach of rehabilitation leads to such a deviation using the case of the Upper Krishna Irrigation Project (UKP) in the northern part of Karnataka, India. Comparative transaction cost reasoning is used to explain this, which emphasizes that when the transaction costs arises due to *ex-post* uncertainties and asset specificities; rehabilitation may be inefficient.

One objective of governance is to protect the interests of the respective parties and adapt the relationship to changing circumstances (Williamson 1987b). As discussed in Section 4.3, a system that minimizes the transaction costs of the farmers in their rehabilitation is more efficient in allocating the property rights (Lueck and Miceli 2004). Monetary compensation is most likely to be efficient in rehabilitation of farmers when costs of finding the land are relatively low. Therefore, we show how specificities related to land characteristics, uncertainties in search for alternatives, and information constrains impose high non-monetary transaction costs on farmers. We use the same analytical framework to make a preliminary assessment of the new draft legislation called the Right to Fair Compensation and Transparency in Land Acquisition, Rehabilitation and Resettlement (RFCTLARR) (Amendment) Ordinance 2015, which replaces the older legislation. We try to gauge whether the new legislation minimizes the burdens of transaction costs on farmers.

Our analysis shows that the R&R procedure in the UKP did not result in the intended outcome of economic rehabilitation despite adequate incentives because of high transaction costs imposed on farmers in search of alternate suitable land. The farmers are exposed to uncertainties due to unforeseen *ex-post* changes. Farmers, before displacement, do not have information about *ex-post* changes of land prices, land availability, location, and quality. These uncertainties are created because of the hybrid mode of governance enacted by the current legislation (LAA 1894) where the state appropriates land as part of a hierarchical system but then leaves 'limitedly informed' farmers in the open market.

A newly proposed legislation intends to address these transaction costs through 'land-for-land' and employment-based provisions but the impact of which can only be assessed in the future.

5 The Role of Access to *de jure* Rights in Resettlement of Displaced Farmers[1]

Overview

A right is accompanied by rules that specify choices a right-holder must make in order to exercise it. The right to claim compensation of land acquisition has rules, which specify two methods of claim – consent method and arbitration method. Does a choice between these affect the benefit stream and if yes, then what factors influence this choice? This chapter aims to answer this question using a binary response model on a primary dataset of displaced farmers from the Upper Krishna Irrigation Project, India. It validates 'access based' hypotheses in choice of compensation and test whether in addition to allocated property rights, benefits actually depend on 'access' to those rights. Results suggest that the choice is governed by access to political bargaining power and information. Therefore, farmers lacking these fail to get resettled despite the presence of a policy framework aimed at their rehabilitation.

5.1 Introduction

In most of the countries, regulatory control over property rights of privately owned land rests in the hands of the government (Doremus 2003; Jacobs 2006; Lueck and Miceli 2007). The government redistributes (gives or takes away) the land property rights of the owners depending upon a specific context (Bromley 1991). Physical 'takings'[2] or land acquisition has gained importance in developing countries like India as it happens often for developmental projects by the government. It is inevitable for the landholders, especially farmers to forego their rights over land for such developmental projects because the state holds the right to acquire private land at any time for development purposes. This is called a right of the *eminent domain* (Jacobs 2006; Lueck and Miceli 2007; Epstein 2012). This shift in property rights causes disruptions which are socio-cultural, economic, and physical in nature from the perspective of the landowners. As a result, impoverishment and marginalization in various forms is common in large scale displacement by development projects, especially dams and irrigation projects (Terminski 2013). Various forms of marginalization occur in terms of shrinking asset holdings, fall in income, and a reduced standard of living. This

---

[1] This chapter is presented at: 1) 19th Annual Conference of The International Society for New Institutional Economics (ISNIE), June 18-20, 2015, Harvard University in Cambridge, Massachusetts; 2) Workshop, Russian Summer School on Institutional Analysis, June 28 – July 4, 2014, Moscow, Russia. This chapter has been submitted to Journal of Development Studies, which is under review process.
[2] A physical 'takings' is an appropriation of the property rights of a whole or a part of privately owned land for development projects (Epstein 2012).

occurs despite the fact that respective governments are obliged to compensate and rehabilitate affected people as per the provisions of *eminent domain* or rehabilitation policies. The desired outcome of such compensation and rehabilitation is to improve or at least re-instate the income level and standard of living of displaced people (Cernea 2003). Rehabilitation policies of some developing countries implicitly assume that monetary compensation is sufficient to achieve the intended outcome of rehabilitation (Cernea 2003). However, it has been argued that despite such compensation provisions, affected people end up worse-off or become impoverished after displacement (Fischel and Shapiro 1989; Cernea 1998, 2003). The researchers have identified several possible causes of impoverishment – a) compensation centered rehabilitation policy (only lump-sum payment) with no effort on income/employment restoration; b) too low compensation amount; c) loss of social capital after displacement; and d) poor commitment of the projects in implementing rehabilitation program (Cernea 2003; Kanbur 2003; Cernea 2004; De Wet 2006a; Mathur 2006c; Singh 2012).

In a developing country like India, the government, in case of land acquisition, compensates the farmers a monetary payment through two methods. The farmers can claim their compensation either through consent method (with the government) or through arbitration method. As discussed in Section 1.4, the consent method is called the Consent Award (CA), where the government decides the amount of compensation to be provided to the farmers. The compensation amount is decided based on the registered value of land in the vicinity but has no scope for arbitration. The arbitration method is called the General Award (GA). It has been argued that the estimation method of land price under the CA is flawed and unscientific as land prices are starkly under-stated in the registered sale deeds (Ministry of Rural Development 1996; Vyas and Mahalingam 2011; Singh 2012; Bose 2013). Singh (2012) analyses the cases of judicial arbitrations dealing with compensation in Delhi, Punjab, and Haryana. He finds that 86 per cent of arbitrations in Delhi courts and 97 per cent in Punjab and Haryana High courts succeeded in claiming higher compensation than that provided in the CA. On an average, compensation claimed through arbitration was 200 per cent higher.

The evaluation report of arbitration cases of the Upper Krishna Project (UKP) during 1993 shows that compensation amount through the GA increased on an average by 37 per cent over the CA (World Bank 1998). These cases illustrate that landowners have a strong incentive to claim their compensation through the GA. In that case, why do all the landholders who face land acquisition not claim their compensation through the arbitration method? For instance, in one of the irrigation projects in Karnataka (India) - UKP, only 10-20 per cent of landholders who lost their land rights claimed their compensation through the arbitration method. Why did the majority of the landholders claim their compensation through the CA? Do the farmers willingly consent with the compensation amount provided in the CA? Singh (2012) and Asif (1999) explain that the large land holdings and other asset holdings are the main determinants of choosing the GA. However, the author argues that not only the wealth of farmers but also other factors of 'access' influence farmers' decision in choosing the methods of compensation claim.

The rest of the chapter is structured as follows: Section 5.2 describes in detail the issue of land acquisition and rehabilitation and its institutional arrangements. the existing literature on land acquisition and rehabilitation problems is also discussed here. Section 5.3 reviews and discusses the theoretical basis of an *access*-based approach to property rights, which emphasizes that factors of access affect the intended outcome(s). Primary data collection and the empirical design applied to the UKP compensation claims are described in Section 5.4. Section 5.5 presents the results and a discussion while Section 6 concludes with policy implications.

5.2 Institutions for Land Acquisition and Rehabilitation

5.2.1 Development Projects and Displacement Scenario

Land, especially in regions with high population density, has a conflicting claim. It is a limited natural resource for the inhabitants, but is also prime input for societal development projects like dams and irrigation projects, road and rail infrastructure, urban development, and industrial zones. For these to be implemented, vast amount of agricultural, common grazing and forestlands are physically 'taken' from the holders. Because of such land use conversion, private land holders need to be displaced. An earlier estimate indicates that each year, around 10-15 million people are involuntarily displaced as a consequence of these development projects worldwide (Stanley 2000). Indeed, this excludes large number of minor projects' displacement, inclusion of which will raise the figures drastically. Dams and irrigation projects alone contribute 40 per cent ($\approx$ 5-6 million) of the total population displaced per year by the development projects (Stanley 2004). Estimates indicate that World Bank irrigation projects accounted for 13 million displaced people till the year 1993, which was 66 per cent of total population displaced due to several World Bank projects (Stanley 2000). Of these, significant contribution (52 per cent) was in South Asia, where India was the largest country involving many irrigation projects with commensurate displacement (Stanley 2000).

Estimates also indicate that since independence (i.e., 1947), approximately 60 million people have been displaced in India due to development projects, out of which 40 per cent are tribal (Choudhury 2013). However, according to the Indian Ministry of Rural Development (1996) and Shah (2010), this is a conservative estimate – the actual number may be high. Despite such high numbers, displacement may not be a social problem if rehabilitation and resettlement (R&R) are just. Incidentally, the laws on land acquisition have not been very successful in rehabilitating and resettling the displaced people (Asif 1999; Bose 2013;

Choudhury 2013). Land acquisition and rehabilitation is a complicated process as it involves social, economic, and cultural disruptions of communities after displacement. Despite the compensation provision, development-induced displacement and rehabilitation faces severe institutional challenges across the world.

5.2.2 Institutional Perspective of Land Acquisition and Rehabilitation

In spite of all the efforts, land acquisition and rehabilitation are still the strongest challenges in the implementation of development projects (Vyas and Mahalingam 2011). Many R&R programs often face a variety of impoverishment risks especially for the vulnerable who do not have the power and voice (Cernea 1997; Fernandes 1998; Mathur 2006c). The displaced are often already poor and might end-up further worse-off for a long period after displacement (Cernea 1997; Kanbur 2003). In this process, they also face complex socio-economic and cultural problems (De Wet 2006a). This is mainly because of the weak institutional arrangements and their enforcement mechanism in the rehabilitation program (Mathur 2006c).

In most cases of land acquisition across world, monetary means of compensation is a common method for compensating landowners. Vyas and Mahalingam (2011) identified three general principles of compensation in land acquisition. They are: "value to the owner", "just compensation" and "reasonable compensation". The "value to the owner" principle of compensation takes into account land value and other tangible and intangible benefits attached to it by considering socio-economic aspects of land use change. In Australia, Hong Kong and most of the other Commonwealth countries, this principle is followed in private land acquisition for development projects (Vyas and Mahalingam 2011). The "just compensation" principle is oriented mainly towards monetary compensation with the criteria that the landowners should be made better-off *ex-post* land acquisition. This principle is followed in countries like India, US, Germany, Italy, Philippines, Brazil, and Cambodia (ADB 2007; Vyas and Mahalingam 2011). Whereas, in the "reasonable compensation" principle, landowners are liable only for their direct losses, where any other benefits attached to land are not considered. Countries like China and states like British Columbia (in Canada) follow this principle (Vyas and Mahalingam 2011).

There are four different compensation estimation methods of land acquisition, which are widely applied across the world (ADB 2007; Vyas and Mahalingam 2011). The first is a 'market-based' approach in which the compensation is estimated based on either sales of land in nearby places (registered sale deeds) or the cost involved in replacing the similar land (replacement value). This approach is commonly employed in India, US, Germany, Italy, Great Britain, and Malaysia. By considering post-acquisition externalities, countries like India, Germany, Great Britain, Italy and others also pay higher compensation or some extra solatium other than the estimated compensation. The second is the 'net value of income from land' approach, which is employed in countries like Tanzania, where land markets either do not exist or skewed. The approach is based on the present value of the future income stream expected from the property. Although this approach is effective where the land market is distorted or inactive, it is associated with serious flaws. The number of years to be considered in calculating the total present value of the future stream of income from the land is always ambiguous. Besides, the uncertainty of future costs and returns is another problem of the approach.

Table 5-1: Different approaches of compensation estimation

Sl. No.	Method	Characteristics	Valuation approach	Country of practice
1	Market based approach	Land tittles and transactions registered	Based on registered sale deeds of replacement value	India, US, Germany, Italy, Great Britain, and Malaysia
2	Net value of income from land approach	Land market inactive	Present value of future income stream of property	Tanzania
3	Original land use value Approach	Land market absent	Agriculture as original use in rural areas	China
4	Consensus approach	Discourse with land owners	Decentralized and participatory	Peru, Singapore and Japan

Source: Own Compilation based on ADB (2007) and Vyas and Mahalingam (2011)

The third is the approach of 'original land use value' as set by the State. China follows this approach as there is hardly any land market existing because of the prohibition of voluntary transfer of farmland to others by owners (Chan 2003). 'Original use' is undefined and in most of the cases, especially in rural areas, agriculture is considered as the original use of land often ignoring other profitable use. The fourth and the last approach is the 'consensus approach', a decentralized participatory approach, where, compensation is estimated / finalized through conducting discourses with landowners. Countries like Peru, Singapore, and Japan follow this approach. Table 5-1 shows the key differences and other characteristics of these four methods. With this background, the next sub-section describes the land acquisition and displacement scenario in India.

5.2.3 Land Acquisition and Rehabilitation in India

Currently 57 per cent of total population in India is dependent on agricultural and allied activities for their livelihood as compared to higher figures a couple of decades earlier (Tripathi and Prasad 2009; India 2011b). As a result, acquisition of land for development projects requires displacement of a large number of people. Because of the fragmented nature of land holdings, the density of farmers and farm labor is usually high, which makes the land acquisition process even more complicated (Marjit 2010). Land acquisition and rehabilitation in India is governed by the doctrine of *eminent domain* as contained in the Land Acquisition Act (LAA) 1894. The LAA, 1894 has been criticized for being ineffective as far as the rehabilitation component goes and has also been termed undemocratic and anti-landowner (Asif 1999; Bose 2013; Choudhury 2013). It also lacks consensus and participation (Vyas and Mahalingam 2011). There is hardly any provision of negotiation with owners; the process of acquisition and compensation is slow and the method of compensation estimation controversial. Rent seeking, bureaucracy, and enforcement problems further make it ineffective (Pandey and Morris 2007; Debnath 2008; Vyas and Mahalingam 2011).

With all these lacuna, the Act poses an enhanced risk of impoverishment and marginalization of landowners in many cases (Cernea 1990; Fernandes 1998). This is well substantiated by evidence as several studies have found that under the current rehabilitation framework of the LAA, farmers marginalized from medium to small and small to below poverty line post-displacement (Parasuraman 1996; Desai et al. 2007). Hence, in order to hasten the process of acquisition so as not to delay the project implementation and provide more choices to farmers, the Government of India (GoI) initiated an award scheme, where compensation is decided based on the farmers' consent (CA). And those who do not comply with consent are provided the option of arbitration (GA). As mentioned already in Section 5.1, there are strong incentives to opt for the GA method, as the compensation amount is very high. Yet, farmers often choose the CA and end up with lower compensation. Before trying to answer why this is so, it is important to understand that de jure rights could be rendered ineffective by factors preventing their exercise.

5.3 Property Rights and Access

The property rights-based approach has been widely applied in studying the incentives and the conflicts associated with the natural resource (especially land) use and allocation. Property rights are understood in several ways in literature, i.e., legal property rights and economic property rights (Barzel 1997; Cole and Grossman 2002; Musole 2009). In legal terms, property rights are relations between people respecting things, which indicate the legally enforceable authority of one or group of persons against at least one other person (Cole and Grossman 2002; Musole 2009). Bromley (1991: 2) defines property right as 'a claim to a benefit stream that the state agrees to protect by assigning the duty to others' (Bromley 1991: 2). Rights are accompanied by two kinds of duties - one for others to respect the rights and the other to the right-holder, which restricts the use of rights in particular ways. Rights, in this sense, are the authority assigned to a person over some 'thing', which are defined and enforced by the state (Feder and Feeny 1991; Barzel 1997; Ostrom and Hess 2008; Musole 2009). Whereas, economic property rights that an individual has over a commodity (or an asset) stand for the abilities of the individual to realize benefits from the asset (Barzel 1997). Barzel (1997) elaborates further the two concepts as 'economic rights are the end (that is, what people ultimately seek), whereas legal rights are the means to achieve the end'. The literature on property rights has mostly dealt with distribution of property rights and property regimes for efficient resource allocation and use (Libecap 1986, 1989; Schlager and Ostrom 1992; Libecap 1993; Cole 2010).

However, land or any resource usually is the object of several different rights, which are often referred to in the literature as a bundle of rights (Alchian and Demsetz 1973; Schlager and Ostrom 1992). Alchian and Demsetz (1973) describe them as exclusivity, inheritability, transferability, and enforcement mechanisms. Libecap (1989) defines them as right to use, right to earn income from, and right to transfer or exchange the assets and resources. Whereas, Schlager and Ostrom (1992) describe them as use rights (access and withdrawal), management rights, exclusion rights, and alienation rights. In case of land under private property regime, the right holders do have all these bundle of rights. Yet another right, especially in case of land and much discussed in the 'takings' literature, is the right to *claim compensation* (Miceli and Segerson 2000; Bell and Parchomovsky 2001; Doremus 2003; Epstein 2012; Singh 2012). The private land holders do have this right to claim compensation whenever all other land rights are involuntarily taken by the government for development purpose (physical 'takings' or land acquisition). This is observed in many parts of the world, which is legitimized under the eminent domain clause. This right has a temporal and frequency dimension, which gives the holder the right to claim compensation only once at the time of acquisition.

Schlager and Ostrom (1992), in their theoretical explanation of property rights, differentiate 'rights' and 'rules', and prescribe that the rules authorize or specify the requirements a right holder must meet in order to exercise the particular right. They provide an illustration – if a fisherman has a right to fish there could be rules that specify the requirements he should meet before he is allowed to fish, which could be related to the specific instruments and methods to be used for fishing. Meinzen-Dick (2014) calls these rules the right-holders' duties or responsibilities. In this sense, the government designs rules that authorize and specify the land owners the ways to exercise the right to claim compensation. In some cases, persons are able to realize the benefits from a resource even without having formal or informal rights (Meinzen-Dick 2014). Pradhan and Pradhan (2000) analyze such a context in Nepal, where some of the farmers who do not have rights to withdraw are able to withdraw water for irrigation. The authors list some of the factors of access to water for irrigation to these farmers. They could be force, stealth or negotiation with those who have rights or they could be political or administrative bargaining power. In contrast, the right holders sometimes may not be able to realize an intended benefit stream from a particular resource even after they have been assigned property rights. For instance, farmers may have land rights but may not be able to achieve the intended benefits because they have no physical access to land or access to labor or capital (Ribot and Peluso 2003). Franco (2008), while analyzing peasants' legal land rights claim makings in the Philippines, asserts how claiming the land rights remain difficult for the peasants despite having more specialized legal resources. Hence, legal rights are *necessary* but not *sufficient* to derive benefits from resources (Bogale and Korf 2007).

Property rights are *de jure* when those rights are lawful or legal by government and are *de facto* when they are formed among resource users (Schlager and Ostrom 1992). However, rights as formal institutional arrangements are only one of the several factors to access and use of resources (Mearns and Binns 1995). Compared to the de jure property rights, *access* is a broad concept which includes both "de jure" and "de facto or extra-legal" rights (Ribot 1998). *Access* puts property rights as one set of mechanisms under a broad range of institutional, social and political relations that influence the benefit stream (Ribot and Peluso 2003). Ribot and Peluso (2003) therefore state that *access* is more akin to a "bundle of power" than to a "bundle of rights." It also argues that since the term access is defined as the 'freedom or ability to obtain or make use of', it is more about *ability,* an inherent characteristic independent of social or legal approval, whereas the term *rights* hinges on societal support (Ribot 1998; Merriam-Webster 2004: 7).

Thus the related concept of *'functionings'* and *'capability'* further strengthens the access based arguments for property rights distribution (Sen 2008). According to Sen, *'functionings* represent parts of the state of a person – in particular the various things that he or she manages to do or be in leading a life' (*ibid.*). 'The *capability* of a person reflects the alternative combinations of functionings the person can achieve, and from which he or she can choose one collection' (*ibid.*). A variety of factors including personal characteristics and social arrangements determine the capability of a person (*ibid.*). Franco (2008) finds the factors of access, to claim legal land rights through political-legal mobilization, as acquisition of information, 'rights-advocacy' and an integrated social movement strategy.

In the context of this thesis, farmers' ability to generate their livelihood and income depends on their access to resources and their ability to control and use them effectively (Berry 1989). Therefore, it looks into the specific factors of *access* and not simply considers *rights* that influence the farmers' decision in choosing the GA method of compensation claim. The next section elaborates on model specification, the choice of access variables, survey design and the hypotheses.

5.4 Empirical Strategy

5.4.1 Dichotomous Choice (Probit) Model

A dichotomous choice model (probit) is used to estimate the factors influencing choice of compensation-claim awards with the CA as a base category (set to 0) and the GA as a main category (set to 1).

$$Choice\ of\ Award = \alpha + \beta_i X_{ij} + \gamma_k Z_{kj} + u_j \tag{1}$$

Where α, β_i and γ_k are unknown parameters and u is the residual. A claim is latent variable and is defined as: Choice of Award = 1 if farmer prefers the GA; and 0 otherwise. X is a vector of i access variables having direct influence on the claim-type, where Z is a vector of k control variables.

Unlike in linear regression models, in case of probit the slope coefficients are not described as marginal effects of change in explanatory variables. This is because dichotomous choice models, like probit, take nonlinear functions. Hence, marginal effects at mean are calculated to describe likelihood of choosing the GA when there is small change in a particular explanatory variable, keeping other variables at their mean.

5.4.2 Variables

The bundle of *access* mechanisms which potentially influence the choice of the awards are wealth, information, social identity and access to third party actors like lawyers, leaders, and relatives and friends.[3] Land holding is the key indicator of wealth in rural areas, which could influence farmers' decision. Information about the procedures involved in the CA and the GA (for example, the time and cost involved) could have an influence on farmers' decisions. It may be that information creates more awareness among farmers but it also may create some confusion. Leadership in political party or panchayat and/or membership of any government or cooperative body are manifestation of social identity, which helps in building networks and influence the compensation amount

---

[3] The author was also careful about simultaneity problem between choice of awards and access variables while designing the questionnaire. It may be true that once a farmer chooses the GA, he may seek some more information and may try to contact a third party for further process of compensation claim. But the concern in the study is to test whether having access to any of these access mechanisms, **before or while choosing the awards,** influence farmers' decision to the GA but not after the award has been chosen. Accordingly, questions were posed to farmers regarding their access to these modes. For instance, did the farmers have the information about the CA and the GA while choosing the award? Was a farmer member of any of the categories when he made his decision? Was a farmer influenced by any person to make the decision about the choice? If yes, who has influenced the most? What was his land holding at the time of choosing the award or before submergence? Data about control variables are also ex-ante to the decisions.

through proper decision making. Third party actors, which include lawyers and leader, and government officials, relatives and friends, could also influence the farmers' choice decision. Government officials try to influence the farmers' decision to prefer the CA by conducting the group meetings (*Gram Sabhas*) so that delays in project implementation can be avoided. Lawyers, on the contrary, may try to influence the farmers' decision in a way that serves their vested interests. The third party variable is constructed in such a way that it creates exclusivity. The categories in third party influence are - no influence, influence by lawyers and leaders, and influence by government officials and/or relatives and friends. These were given to respondents and they were asked to select the one that influenced most. This way of eliciting the response makes the categories of the variable exclusive.

Percentage of total land submerged, family type, age, main occupation, caste, previous experience, family size, number of adult members in a family, and per cent of loan to income are used as control variables as they influence the farmers' decision of choosing the award. Percentage of total land submerged affects income of a farmer in different proportions, which in turn may influence his decision. Education level of head of the household, previous experiences with compensation and caste could also influence farmers' decision (Mahapatra and Mitchell 2001; Vanslembrouck et al. 2002; Sheikh et al. 2003; Edwards-Jones 2006). Education of a farmer influences access to legal systems and procedures, which could impact on his decision. Farmers having previous experience in choosing the awards are well aware of pros and cons of each award, which influence their current decision. Farmers of major castes[4] having a good network and resources are more likely to choose the GA.

Family type, age of household head and per cent of loan vis-a-vis income could also influence the farmers' decision (Mahapatra and Mitchell 2001; Zbinden and Lee 2005; Deressa et al. 2009). As non-liquid assets become liquid after land transfer, joint families are more prone to be divided and become nuclear. In addition, even if families do not divide assets immediately, planning differs between joint families and nuclear families[5] due to their size, which could influence the decision. As the age of a household head increases, the degree of risk aversion goes up and similarly with increase in the loan to income ratio, the risk aversion of a farmer increases. In such case, the farmers would prefer the CA. Occupation, size of family and the number of adult members in the family could also play a role in decision making (Zbinden and Lee 2005; Deressa et al. 2009). Landowners with different landholdings and employment

---

[4]   Major castes in the study area are Lingayats, Reddy and Brahmins, which are more educated and comparatively wealthy. Whereas, scheduled castes, scheduled tribes and other backward castes and people belonging to Muslim religion are clubbed in minor castes category. They are relatively poor and poorly educated and also form the minority.

[5]   Nuclear families are also called as elementary families which comprise only of parents and their children.

activities like laborer, business, etc. will be associated with different attitudes towards compensation claims. As family size increases, its dependency on land increases hence making the choice of claim award very important. The *access* mechanisms and the control variables discussed above and their likely effect to go for the GA are listed in Table 5-2.

Besides these, there are possibilities that there may be unobserved characteristics of farmers (representing ability and motivation) influencing the choice of the GA. Some of the control variables used represent ability (*LAND_HOLDING, EDUCATION*, etc.) and some proxy for motivation (*LOAN_TO_INCOME, LAND_SUBMERGED*, etc.). There exists sufficient literature suggesting that these proxies represent abilities and motivation. Huffman (1974), while analyzing farmers' allocative ability in inputs, finds that education and information are indicators to acquire and process the information efficiently. Öhlmér et al. (1998) observe the effect of information and farm size on farmer's perceptive ability and information processing ability. Ali and Kumar (2011) empirically show that education and landholding are among the variables that influence decision-making capabilities of farmers in various farming practices. McElwee and Smith (2012) examine the role farmer's personal and farm characteristics on the capability of farmers. Hence, *LAND_HOLDING, INFORMATION, EDUCATION*, and *MEMBERSHIP* variables indicate the ability of the farmers. Similarly, the variables, *LOAN_TO_INCOME* and *LAND_SUBMERGED* represent the motivation of farmers. As percentage of loan to income increases, the risk of farmers in choosing the GA increases and as a result, farmers could prefer the CA option. If the proportion of land submerged is not very high then the farmer could choose either the GA option as he has enough unsubmerged land that is sufficient to sustain his income or choose the CA option as he could improve the remaining land with compensation. Similarly, if the proportion of land submerged is high then also the farmer could either choose the CA or the GA depending upon his situation to sustain and whether he wants to continue with agriculture or not.

Table 5-2: Description of independent variables and hypotheses

Variable	Description
LAND_HOLDING	Total land holding before submergence (acres) (+)
INFORMATION	Awareness about the CA and the GA;=1 if yes (+); and 0 otherwise (-)
MEMBERSHIP	Access to social identity (membership in any government, political party or any other organizations); = 0 if no membership (-); =1 if member of federation/co-operative (+); =2 if member of political party/panchayat (+))
THIRD_PARTY_INFLUENCE	Third party influence; = 0 if no influence (-); =1 if lawyers and leaders (+); =2 if government officials and relatives and friends (+/-)
LAND_SUBMERGED	Per cent of total land submerged (%) (+/-)
EDUCATION	Years of education of household head (+)
FAMILY_TYPE	Family structure / type before displacement; = 1 if joint (-); and 0 if nuclear (+)
AGE_OF_HOUSEHOLD_HEAD	Age of household head (years) (-)
OCCUPATION	Main occupation; = 0 if labor and agriculture (+/-); = 1 if non-agriculture (business and job (+))
CASTE	Caste; = 1 if family belongs to major caste system (+) and 0 otherwise (-)
PREVIOUS_EXPERIENCE	Previous experience in choosing the awards; = 1 if any choice made in the past (+); and 0 otherwise (-/+)
FAMILY_SIZE	Family size (number of family members) (+/-)
ADULTS	Number of adult members in a family (+/-)
LOAN_TO_INCOME	Loan to income (percentage) (-)

Note: '+' and '-' symbols in the parentheses indicates likely effect of variable

The final model for the choice of compensation-claiming awards is formulated as:

$$Pr\,(CHOICE\_AWRD = 1|x) = \Phi\,(\alpha + \beta_1 LAND\_HOLDING$$
$$+\beta_2 INFORMATION + \beta_3 MEMBERSHIP +$$
$$\beta_4 THIRD\_PARTY\_INFLUENCE + \gamma_1 LAND\_SUBMERGED +$$
$$\gamma_2 EDUCATION + \gamma_3 FAMILY\_TYPE + \gamma_4 AGE\_OF\_HOUSEHOLD\_HEAD$$

$+ \gamma_5 \text{OCCUPATION} + \gamma_6 \text{CASTE} + \gamma_7 \text{PREVIOUS\_EXPERIENCE} +$
$\gamma_8 \text{FAMILY\_SIZE} + \gamma_9 \text{ADULTS} + \gamma_{10} \text{LOAN\_TO\_INCOME})$

Table 5-3 indicates that compensation is higher through the GA than that through the CA irrespective of whether the land is irrigated or rainfed. Average compensation for irrigated and rainfed under the GA are around 4 times and 1.2 times higher than that of the CA respectively.

Table 5-3: **Compensation amount per acre (Rs. thousand) claimed by survey farmers under both the awards**

Particulars	General Award (GA)		Consent Award (CA)		GA/CA	GA/CA
	Irrigated land	Dry land	Irrigated land	Dry land	Irrigated land	Dry land
Average	450*	91*	115	76	3.91	1.20
Minimum	140	40	49	3	2.86	13.33
Maximum	3000	120	148	87	20.24	1.38

Note: * indicates that the difference between compensation amounts under the GA and the CA is statistically significant (t-test) for both irrigated land and dry land.

Source: Own computation from the survey data

5.4.3 Sampling Design

The fieldwork for this study was conducted in the submerged area of the UKP, located in Bagalkot district of Karnataka state, India (Figure 5-1). Average annual rainfall in the submerged area is 562 millimeters (mm) against the state's average rainfall of 1139mm (GoK). In the submerged area, 70 per cent of agricultural land has deep or very deep black soils, most of which has surface and/or groundwater irrigation (GoK 2006). Majority of the population (90 per cent) in the submerged area is dependent on agriculture and allied activities as against the district's average of 70 per cent (GoK 2006; Census 2011a). Literacy rate in the submerged area is 54.5 per cent as against the district's literacy of 57 per cent (Census 2011a). Average income of households of the sample is Rs. 12,407, which is nearly half of the district's per capita income of Rs. 21,980 (Shiddalingaswami and Raghavendra 2010). In a nutshell, the affected population is in dry region with low per capita income and high dependence on agriculture.

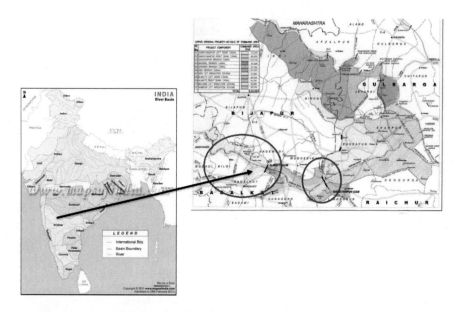

Figure 5-1: Geographical location of Upper Krishna Project

Source: (MoI 2012; GoK 2014).

A primary survey is done to collect data from the displaced farmers through stratified random sampling in seven selected villages of Bagalkot district, over a period of four months during the year 2013. Table 5-4 shows distribution of farmers surveyed from each of these seven villages. A sample of 199 farmers is interviewed to have nearly equal representation of farmers with both the claims – the GA (90 farmers) and the CA (109 farmers).

Table 5-4: Village wise sample collection

Sl. No	Village	Consent Award (CA)	General Award (GA)	Total interviews
1	Anadinni	17 (77)	5 (23)	22
2	Haveli	7 (41)	10 (59)	17
3	Kadampur	13 (62)	8 (38)	21
4	Kesnur	11 (79)	3 (21)	14
5	Murnal	32 (55)	26 (45)	58
6	Veerapur	13 (30)	30 (70)	43
7	Yadahalli	16 (67)	8 (33)	24
	Total	**109 (55)**	**90 (45)**	**199**

Note: Figures in the parentheses indicate percentage to total.

Source: Own compilation

Table 5-5: Summary statistics of independent variables

Variable	General Award (GA) (N= 90)			Consent Award (CA) (N=108)			t test
	Observations	Mean	SD	Observations	Mean	SD	(P val.)
LAND_HOLDING	90	8.05	7.45	108	7.44	6.61	0.54
INFORMATION*	90	0.38	0.49	108	0.18	0.39	0.00
MEMBERSHIP	90	0.17	0.43	108	0.08	0.36	0.11
MEMBERSHIP_0 (No membership)	77			102			
MEMBERSHIP_1(Member of federation/co-operative)	11			3			
MEMBERSHIP_2 (Member of political party/panchayat)	02			3			
THIRD_PARTY_INFLUENCE	90	0.90	1.02	108	0.68	1.34	0.20
THIRD_PARTY_INFLUENCE_0 (No influence)	32			83			
THIRD_PARTY_INFLUENCE_1 (Lawyers and leaders)	53			4			
THIRD_PARTY_INFLUENCE_2 (Government officials, and relatives and friends)	5			21			
LAND_SUBMERGED	90	67.67	34.84	108	64.06	31.94	0.44
EDUCATION	90	5.52	4.39	108	5.45	4.48	0.54
FAMILY_TYPE*	90	0.61	0.49	108	0.78	0.41	0.00
AGE_OF_HOUSEHOLD_HEAD*	90	41.03	12.88	108	45.78	11.74	0.01
OCCUPATION	90	0.12	0.33	108	0.13	0.59	0.24
CASTE	90	0.74	0.44	108	0.82	0.38	0.17
PREVIOUS_EXPERIENCE*	90	0.26	0.44	108	0.06	0.25	0.00
FAMILY_SIZE*	90	8.72	4.40	108	10.31	6.78	0.05
ADULTS*	90	3.82	1.58	108	6.38	4.56	0.00
LOAN_TO_INCOME	90	1.24	3.46	108	0.73	2.07	0.20

Note: * indicates significant at 5 per cent; Number of observations reduced from 199 to 198 as land holding of one farmer was 6 times of the mean land holding of the sample group and is considered as an outlier; discrete variables with more than two categories (MEMBERSHIP and THIRD_PARTY_INFLUENCE) are not ordered, for which dummies are used.

Before conducting the main survey, a pilot survey of 20 farmers was carried out to pre-test the semi-structured questionnaire. Focus group discussions (FGDs) were conducted to understand the context and gather general information. The questionnaire consisted of crucial information in terms of land and asset holdings, socio-economic and demographic indicators of the farmers, cropping pattern before and after displacement, and detailed information on choice of claiming mechanism and compensation.[1] Table 5-5 shows descriptive statistics of the

---

[1]   Questionnaire is available from authors on request.

explanatory variables for the two groups – farmers opting the GA vs farmers choosing the CA. The mean comparison shows that farmers going for the GA have high information, their household head is younger, and have previous experience and have large family size and the differences are statistically significant.

5.5 Empirical Results and Discussion

5.5.1 Results

The different probit models were run to estimate the likelihood of choosing the GA. Table 5-6 reports the results. Except land holding (*LAND_HOLDING*) other main explanatory variables are categorical and thus are introduced as dummy variables. Similarly, the dummies were introduced for control variables like family type (*FAMILY_TYPE*), main occupation of household head (*OCCUPATION*), caste (*CASTE*), and previous experience in choosing the awards (*PREVIOUS_EXPERIENCE*).

In the first model, all the explanatory variables that can influence the choice of the awards were included (i.e., equation 2). Given the fact that a large family (*FAMILY_SIZE*) tends to have more adult members (*ADULTS*), including both *FAMILY_SIZE* and *ADULTS* would make the estimates inconsistent due to muticollinearity. Accordingly, *FAMILY_SIZE* variable was dropped in the second model. Moreover, it is not the family size, rather adult members that influence the decision of choosing the claiming rights, thus *ADULTS* is better representative of decision making. Spearman correlation coefficients at 5 per cent significance, with Bonferroni adjustment, show a high correlation between *INFORMATION* & *EDUCATION* (Years of education of household head), *AGE_OF_HOUSEHOLD_HEAD* & *EDUCATION*, *FAMILY_TYPE* & *ADULTS*, and *FAMILY_TYPE* & *PREVIOUS_EXPERIENCE*. Hence, *EDUCATION* and *FAMILY_TYPE* variables were dropped in the third model.

In the fourth model, the *CASTE* variable is dropped as it was not a significant determinant of compensation choice in earlier models.[2] The significance of both main variables and other explanatory variables however is unaffected. The fourth model thus is the best fit for the sample. P-value of Chi-squared test indicates the overall significance of the model (Table 5-6). The overall rate of correct prediction of fourth model is estimated to be 85 per cent, with 89 per cent of the observations of farmers who have chosen the GA specified correctly (specificity) and 80 per cent of the observations of farmers who have chosen the CA specified correctly (sensitivity) (see Table 5-8, Appendix). Based on the sign and significance, it seems that farmers are more likely to claim compensation through the GA when their land holding (*LAND_HOLDING*) increases. It means

---

[2] The reason for the *CASTE* variable being not significant could be no variation in the data as nearly 80 per cent of the surveyed farmers belong to a single caste.

that the GA is not a feasible alternative for marginal farmers. This is probably because of a) low risk bearing ability of small farmers; and b) the need for immediate liquidity by small farmers. Similarly, sign and significance of the *INFORMATION* suggests that the farmers having information about both the awards are more likely to choose the GA. This is because they have better appreciation about the expected time and cost to claim compensation and thus are able to organize their future economic activities accordingly.

Table 5-6: What determines an award choice? - Probit estimation results

(Dependent Variable CHOICE_AWRD = 1 if farmer choses GA and 0 otherwise)

Variables	MODEL-1	MODEL-2	MODEL-3	MODEL-4
LAND_HOLDING	0.0112	0.0320*	0.0315*	0.0301[#]
	(0.0221)	(0.0192)	(0.0190)	(0.0191)
INFORMATION_1	1.127***	1.023***	1.018***	1.018***
	(0.3093)	(0.291)	(0.2942)	(0.294)
MEMBERSHIP_1	1.288***	1.238***	1.251***	1.234***
	(0.4857)	(0.4696)	(0.4821)	(0.4741)
MEMBERSHIP_2	0.2031	-0.2615	-0.3651	-0.3582
	(0.8915)	(0.9841)	(0.9902)	(0.9780)
THIRD_PARTY_INFLUENCE _1	2.585***	2.373***	2.356***	2.356***
	(0.4022)	(0.3411)	(0.3453)	(0.346)
THIRD_PARTY_INFLUENCE _2	-0.856**	-0.604*	-0.5946	-0.622*
	(0.4001)	(0.3646)	(0.3668)	(0.3650)
LAND_SUBMERGED	0.0017	0.0009	0.0008	0.0014
	(0.0042)	(0.0041)	(0.0041)	(0.0040)
EDUCATION	0.0172	-0.0066		
	(0.0325)	(0.0302)		
FAMILY_TYPE_1	-0.631**	-0.1745		
	(0.2912)	(0.2788)		
AGE_OF_HOUSEHOLD_HEAD	0.0006	-0.0048	-0.0032	-0.0037
	(0.0161)	(0.0129)	(0.0120)	(0.0120)
OCCUPATION_1	-0.0846	-0.2752	-0.2785	-0.3322
	(0.4509)	(0.4330)	(0.4181)	(0.4188)
CASTE_1	-0.0195	-0.2830	-0.3022	
	(0.3436)	(0.3096)	(0.3091)	
PREVIOUS_EXPERIENCE_1	1.645***	1.381***	1.435***	1.394***
	(0.3899)	(0.3754)	(0.3684)	(0.3669)

Table 5-6 continued

Variables	MODEL-1	MODEL-2	MODEL-3	MODEL-4
FAMILY_SIZE	0.234***			
	(0.0558)			
ADULTS	-0.456***	-0.142***	-0.150***	-0.150***
	(0.1025)	(0.0445)	(0.0437)	(0.0432)
LOAN_TO_INCOME	0.0679	0.0936	0.0905	0.0860#
	(0.0525)	(0.0575)	(0.0573)	(0.0543)
Constant	-1.1560	-0.3097	-0.4781	-0.7037
	(0.8961)	(0.7661)	(0.6878)	(0.6798)
Observations	198	198	198	198
Psuedo R-squared	0.586	0.525	0.523	0.5199
Log likelihood	-56.47	-64.86	-65.06	-65.50
Chi-squared	100.4	98.13	90.92	90.15
p-value	0	0	0	0

Notes: Robust standard errors in parentheses; Significance level: ***$p<0.01$, **$p<0.05$, *$p<0.1$, #$p<0.15$.

The social identity of the farmers by means of membership in either federation[3] or co-operative (*MEMBERSHIP_1*) indicates that they would prefer to claim their compensation through the GA.[4] This could be because of the networks these farmers have with government and other legal officials in gaining information and influencing the claiming process to gain higher compensation. In addition to these variables, third party influence is also considered to analyze role of lawyers and leaders (*THIRD_PARTY_INFLUENCE_1)*, and government officials, relatives and friends (*THIRD_PARTY_INFLUENCE_2)* in influencing the farmers' decision. Lawyers and leaders (*THIRD_PARTY_INFLUENCE_1*) influenced the farmers' decision significantly in claiming compensation through the GA as they have the greater incentive if the claim is achieved through arbitration. The FGDs with farmers also revealed that lawyers persuaded several farmers to choose the GA by paying them some amount in advance, which was equal to or slightly higher than the CA amount. However, government officials,

---

[3] Federation is a type of organization like, milk federation, fruit growers associations, etc.

[4] In case of *MEMBERSHIP*, it was specifically asked in the survey that whether a farmer was member of more than one category. Any non-exclusive observations were not observed in the data, where a farmer is a member of both the categories (member of federation/co-operative and member of political party/panchayat). Still, this may be a possibility and to avoid bias and to create exclusivity, the categories were merged and made it binary (= 1 if a farmer is a member in any of these categories and = 0 otherwise) and ran the probit model. However, little difference was found in the results.

relatives, and friends (*THIRD_PARTY_INFLUENCE_2*) negatively influenced the farmers' decision to choose the GA.

Table 5-7 shows the marginal effects of explanatory variables. The marginal effect - in case of continuous variables - explains percentage change in probability of claiming the compensation through the GA for a unit change in an explanatory variable, whereas, in case of categorical variable, marginal effect explains percentage change in probability of claiming the compensation through the GA for variable changing from base category to other category. As the fourth model is the best-fit model, only its results are referred for further discussion. Although the effect of land holding (*LAND_HOLDING*) is positive and significant, it has a mild impact on likelihood of choosing the GA. A unit change in landholding leads to approximately 1 per cent increase in the probability of choosing the GA.[5] Farmers having information (*INFORMATION_1*) about the claim awards are 39 per cent more likely to choose the GA as compared to those who do not have the information. Similarly, for a farmer having social identity through membership in federation / cooperatives (*MEMBERSHIP_1*), the likelihood is more by 43 per cent as compared to those who do not have the social identity. Lawyers and leaders (*THIRD_PARTY_INFLUENCE_1*) as the third party influence have strong influence on the likelihood of farmers choosing the GA (73 per cent) as compared to the farmers who do not have the third party influence. Whereas, farmers influenced by government officials, relatives and friends (*THIRD_PARTY_INFLUENCE_2*) are 23 per cent less likely to choose the GA.

Among the control variables, non-agricultural main occupation (*OCCUPATION_1*) does not appear to have a statistically significant influence on the likelihood of choosing the GA. Farmers having previous experience (*PREVIOUS_EXPERIENCE_1*) have 49 per cent more likelihood of choosing the GA than those who do not have experience of an award. The number of adults in a family (*ADULTS*) has a negative influence on farmers' likelihood of choosing the GA. For every adult member increase in a family, the likelihood of choosing the GA decreases by 6 per cent. This could be due to either plans of family division immediately post-compensation[6] or a pressing need of compensation for consumptive and income generating purpose.

Since discrete choice models often face a risk of having endogenous independent variables, any suspicious 'access variable' having endogeneity problem was checked. It was presumed that *INFORMATION* variable could be possibly endogenous. The IVPROBIT model was run using *EDUCATION* of Household Head as an instrument. However, the Wald test of exogeneity indicated no endogeneity problem. Similarly, for other two access variables – *LAND_HOLDING* and *MEMBERSHIP*, IVPROBIT models were run using

---

[5] The presence of non-linearity with *LAND_HOLDING* variable was also tested by re-estimating the best-fit model (4) using square of the *LAND_HOLDING* variable. However, estimation results (and marginal effects) do not change much.

[6] Survey sample shows that 52 per cent of farmers divided post-compensation.

CASTE as an instrument. In these cases also, Wald test indicated no endogeneity problem. In addition to access variables, any suspicious variables for having endogeneity problem in control variables were also looked and presumed that *PREVIOUS_EXPERIENCE* could be endogenous. IVPROBIT model was run with using *AGE_OF_HOUSEHOLD_HEAD* as an instrument. Besides IVPROBIT models, propensity score matching approach was also attempted. In the first model, *INFORMATION* was used as the treatment variable and in the second, *THIRD_PARTY_INFLUENCE* was used as the treatment variable. Treatment effects of both the variables were significant, like in case of probit model.

Table 5-7: Marginal effect estimates of different probit models

Variables	MODEL-1	MODEL-2	MODEL-3	MODEL-4
LAND_HOLDING	0.0044	0.0127*	0.0125*	0.0119#
	(0.0088)	(0.0076)	(0.0075)	(0.0076)
INFORMATION_1	0.421***	0.388***	0.387***	0.387***
	(0.1001)	(0.0981)	(0.0998)	(0.0997)
MEMBERSHIP_1	0.438***	0.429***	0.433***	0.429***
	(0.1148)	(0.1154)	(0.1179)	(0.1179)
MEMBERSHIP_2	0.0809	-0.1013	-0.1390	-0.1365
	(0.3536)	(0.3682)	(0.3543)	(0.3509)
THIRD_PARTY_INFLUENCE_1	0.758***	0.729***	0.727***	0.727***
	(0.0559)	(0.0554)	(0.0561)	(0.0562)
THIRD_PARTY_INFLUENCE_2	-0.307**	-0.225*	-0.221*	-0.230*
	(0.1191)	(0.1224)	(0.1232)	(0.1210)
LAND_SUBMERGED	0.0007	0.0004	0.0003	0.0006
	(0.0017)	(0.0016)	(0.0016)	(0.0016)
EDUCATION	0.0068	-0.0026		
	(0.0129)	(0.0120)		
FAMILY_TYPE_1	-0.247**	-0.0693		
	(0.1100)	(0.1107)		
AGE_OF_HOUSEHOLD_HEAD	0.0002	-0.0019	-0.0013	-0.0015
	(0.0064)	(0.0051)	(0.0048)	(0.0048)
OCCUPATION_1	-0.0335	-0.1071	-0.1081	-0.1282
	(0.1778)	(0.1639)	(0.1578)	(0.1556)
CASTE_1	-0.0078	-0.1125	-0.1200	
	(0.1367)	(0.1225)	(0.1222)	
PREVIOUS_EXPERIENCE_1	0.537***	0.481***	0.495***	0.485***
	(0.0781)	(0.0933)	(0.0891)	(0.0915)
FAMILY_SIZE	0.0929***			
	(0.0223)			

Table 5-7 continued

Variables	MODEL-1	MODEL-2	MODEL-3	MODEL-4
ADULTS	-0.181***	-0.0562***	-0.0596***	-0.0596***
	(0.0411)	(0.0177)	(0.0174)	(0.0172)
LOAN_TO_INCOME	0.0270	0.0371	0.0359	0.0341#
	(0.0209)	(0.0228)	(0.0227)	(0.0216)
Observations	198	198	198	198

Note: Robust standard errors in parentheses; Significance level: ***p<0.01, **p<0.05, *p<0.1, #p<0.15.

5.5.2 Discussion

The results indicate that total land holding before submergence, information about the CA and the GA, access to social identity and third party influence significantly affect the likelihood of farmers claiming the compensation through the GA. Land holding (*LAND_HOLDING*) is an indicator of wealth of the farmers, which also implies higher risk bearing ability as the GA involves time to claim compensation. Information about the CA and the GA (*INFORMATION*) implies that the farmers are informed about the procedure, cost and time required in each award, which plays an important role in their decision. Social identity (*MEMBERSHIP*) through which one has the network within a society with key actors like other leaders, lawyers and government officials, is also an important factor in choosing the award. All the three variables together validate the hypothesis that those farmers having these *access* mechanisms are able to choose the GA and get higher compensation.

In addition, access to third party sources (*THIRD_PARTY_INFLUENCE*) like lawyers and leaders influences the farmers in choosing the GA. Leaders have networks and information and could be able to assist farmers in claiming the compensation through the GA. For those lacking these mechanisms, the CA is a better option to claim their compensation. Thus, political bargaining power (in terms of wealth, political affiliation, and network) and information are inevitable to gain access to the benefits which can be enhanced through the GA. This implies that having compensation-claim rights alone, is not sufficient to ensure access to judicial arbitration for higher compensation. This insufficiency of legal rights and a wide disparity among the displaced farmers in having access mechanisms led to compensation distributional inequalities and as a result may accentuate marginalization.

5.6 Conclusion and Implications

In this chapter, it is shown that a lack of access to *de jure* property rights produce less than desirable outcomes in the resettlement of displaced farmers. Unlike in the developed world, land holdings are highly fragmented in India and most of the farmers are small holders. In addition, they have minimal alternative skills for their livelihood other than agriculture based activities. In order to hasten the process of acquisition so as not to delay the project implementation, the Indian government has designed two alternative compensation-claiming awards, the CA and the GA. The CA comprises high lump sum amount of compensation but has no scope for arbitration, whereas the GA has low initial compensation but provides a scope for arbitration for higher compensation. The farmers are free to opt for either of them but often choose the option, which makes them worse-off. This study finds that this is determined by differential access to political bargaining power and information. Therefore, farmers lacking access to these end up with less compensation and this explains their further marginalization. An important insight is that farmers need to be included in the decision making processes for resettlement frameworks. In addition, the strengthening the agricultural extension system in the vicinity could also play an important role. It could be done through village level meetings that provide advanced information about the compensation awards, their objectives, and the processes of the R&R. This might give the farmers a collective bargaining power to influence the compensation amounts so that they get higher compensation in the CA itself rather than going for the GA. What is also needed is greater research to elicit farmers' own preferences for resettlement.

Appendix to Chapter 5

Table 5-8: Classification table

Probit model for choice_award			
Classified	---------- True ----------		Total
	D	~ D	
+	72	12	84
-	18	96	114
Total	90	108	198

Classified + if predicted Pr (D) >= .5
True D defined as Choice_award !=0

Sensitivity	Pr (+ ∣ D)	80.00 %
Specificity	Pr (- ∣~D)	88.89 %
Positive predictive value	Pr (D ∣ +)	85.71 %
Negative predictive value	Pr (~D ∣ -)	84.21 %
False + rate for true ~D	Pr (+ ∣~D)	11.11 %
False – rate for true D	Pr (- ∣ D)	20.00 %
False + rate for classified +	Pr (~D ∣ +)	14.29 %
False – rate for classified -	Pr (D ∣ -)	15.79 %
Correctly classified		84.85 %

6 Institutional *Fit* or *Misfit*? A Contingent Ranking Analysis of Compensation Packages for Land Acquisition in India[1]

Overview

Although the role of public participation in the design of the development-induced displacement and rehabilitation (DIDR) of people is considered important, there is hardly any clarity on the means by which the participation influences institutional fit. There is a paucity of literature, which elicits from the affected farmers their preferences about the appropriate institutional design. We address this problem using a contingent ranking experimental approach on a primary dataset of farmers who are going to be displaced in near future due to an irrigation project in India. We show how institutional preference as an indicator of social fit plays an important role in contextualizing the institutional arrangements of the DIDR. The results validate our hypothesis that the farmers, given a choice, would prefer land or employment based compensation over contemporary monetary compensation. This indicates that there is a mismatch between provisions of the contemporary institutional arrangements of the DIDR and expectations of the farmers, which will be an additional argument for institutional reforms in the current framework of compensation.

6.1 Introduction

Predominantly, the designing, planning, and implementation of contemporary institutional arrangements of the development-induced displacement and rehabilitation (DIDR) in India are top down and centralized. These are mostly monetary provisions based on the registered value of the land and houses. The intended outcome of the DIDR is reflected in how well people are resettled economically, socially, and culturally in sustainable way (De Wet 2006b). However, most of the development projects fail to achieve this outcome (Fischel and Shapiro 1989; Cernea 1998, 2003; Kanbur 2003; Cernea 2004; De Wet 2006a; Mathur 2006c; Singh 2012). As a result, displaced people suffer from deterioration of their economic and social status through shrinking assets, reduced income, and a worsened standard of living.

There could be several reasons for this but primarily it is because farmers face high transaction costs of searching land post-displacement and they lack access to methods/awards to claim the compensation (General Award) (see Chapters 4 and 5). Apart from this, some scholars have also highlighted the lack of farmer participation during the policy formation stage (see for example Asif 1999;

---

[1] This chapter is selected for presentation at International Conference on Land Governance for Equitable and Sustainable Development, July 09 -10, 2015, Utrecht, the Netherlands.

Bagchi 2012). Without taking into account the endogenous preferences of farmers, the 'one size fits all' approach is likely to be ineffective in restoring their standard of living because one-sided approaches more often than not restrict the range of choices for the farmers (De Wet 2001). Acknowledging this, a federal level debate has been going on in India to include a 'participation' component in all rehabilitation policies. De Wet (2001) prescribed an open-ended participatory approach for resettlement planning and implementation processes. In the participatory approach, the government can discuss and negotiate based on the preferences of the displaced people. As an alternative to the participatory approach, De Wet (2001) proposes multi-option packages of compensation for displaced people that include lump-sum cash payment, annuities, land for land lost, grain provision for number of years, and employment (De Wet 2001; Cernea 2004). However, there is no clarity on the nature of such participation. The main reason is that there is no study, which elicits from the affected farmers their preferences in regard to the appropriate institutional design. This therefore necessitates a study on farmers' preferences towards compensation.

In this study, we make an attempt to fill this gap by a choice modeling technique of contingent ranking. In this approach, a hypothetical set of alternative options, relevant to the problem at hand, is created to measure the displaced farmers' preferences for the monetary compensation. The contingent ranking experimental model is employed using demographic features of the farmers affecting their choice - age, gender, occupation, landholding, extent of land submergence, education, number of households in a family - as respondent-specific variables. Data comes from a primary survey of 200 farmers sampled randomly from those who were soon to be displaced due to an irrigation project. The interviews were conducted in the Southern Indian state of Karnataka over a period of four months in the year 2012-13. The state has undertaken several irrigation projects, one of which, named the Upper Krishna Irrigation Project (UKP) is currently in its final phase. For details about the UKP, see Section 1.2.

The rest of the Chapter is structured as follows: Section 2 reviews the literature on institutional design of the DIDR, public participation and its role in institutional design. This section also highlights the gaps in the literature and argues that the theory of institutional 'fit' provides a better framework to understand institutional design. In Section 3, the hypothesis, data collection process and contingent ranking experiment are described. Section 4 presents and interprets the results. Section 5 presents a discussion about how farmers' preferences play a role in effective institutional design. Section 6 concludes with policy insights and the scope of future research.

6.2 The Concept of Institutional Fit

6.2.1 A Review of Literature

The core idea of institutional fit, as introduced by Young (2008) and others (Berkes 2007; Folke et al. 2007; Ostrom 2007; Ostrom et al. 2007), is that institutional arrangements and defining characteristics of the problem they address need to be matched for their effectiveness and sustainability. That is, a treatment should be problem specific, where different resource problems or similar resource problems with different causes are treated differently (Cox 2012). This implies that problems dealing with different natural or social systems needs to be treated accordingly. For instance, groundwater depletion problem could have different causes in different areas, namely, high borewell density per unit area, more amount of water extraction per borewell, water intensive cropping pattern in low rainfall area, inefficient irrigation methods leading to high water usage, farmers' inadequate awareness / information level about amount of water to be irrigated to particular crops, low water infiltration due to either type of soil or any other geographical reasons, etc.

Hence, the emphasis should put on the prominent prevailing causes of the problem in particular region. If groundwater is depleting in a region because of high water intensive cropping pattern like rice[2] and irrigation method like flooding, then policy emphasis needs to be on incentivizing either water saving irrigation methods like drip irrigation, SRI (System of Rice Intensification) cultivation technique, etc. or low water intensive crops cultivation. Bromley (2012), while discussing fit, emphasizes that it is not the dearth of institutional arrangements and policy instruments in addressing the governance problems but the lack of political will to invoke them.

There is sufficient literature which has validated theoretically and empirically the importance of institutional fit in addressing the problem of governing socio-ecological systems (SES) (Ekstrom and Young 2009; Vatn and Vedeld 2012; DeCaro and Stokes 2013; Zikos and Roggero 2013). Referring to Young's concept of institutional fit, Haller et al. (2013) describe fit as the local actors' capacity to design institutions and to cope with problems they address in a particular context. They examine institutional fit and misfit of four cases of floodplain[3] contexts within the changing political economy of pre- and post-colonial Africa, namely Zambia, Cameron, and Tanzania (two cases). Through these cases, they describe the co-evolutionary process of institutional fit and misfit and highlight important features like flexible institutions, leadership, and mutual economic benefit as driving factors to attain fit.

---

[2] In some parts of India (in the state of Andhra Pradesh), rice is irrigated using groundwater.

[3] A floodplain is an area of land adjacent to a stream or river that stretches from the banks of its channel to the base of the enclosing valley walls and experiences flooding during periods of high discharge.

The institutional fit has a characteristic of multidimensionality. Herrfahrdt-Pähle (2010), while analyzing river basin management institutions in South Africa, focuses on the various dimensions of fit, especially spatial fit, functional fit and dynamic fit. By focusing on spatial fit, he emphasizes the problems of boundaries, stakeholder participation, and financial viability as potential causes of misfit. Moss (2012) explores conceptualization and practice of spatial fit in the EU Water Framework Directive and employs the concept in one of the Rhine river sub-basins and pays attention to the political dimension of spatial fit in water management. Nielsen et al. (2013), in their comparative analysis of six countries around the Baltic Sea, analyze the fit of institutional arrangements of water management and find predominantly a top-down approach in most of the cases with hardly any local influence. However, they find that only those cases, which employed the concept of spatial fit, accomplished the local influence. Recently, Mann and Absher (2014) validate political dimension - power structures, values and interests of the concerned actors - to the concept of institutional fit.

In addition to above discussed dimensions, institutional fit has also other dimensions like social, technological, resource, etc. Vatn and Vedeld (2012) criticize Young's position of fit because of its lack of clarity given to relationships between human agency, normativity, and design of institutions as a social process. DeCaro and Stokes (2013) argue that the concept of institutional fit does not take into account the means of public participation influencing policy outcomes. They also point out the ambiguity of the concept of institutional fit regarding constituents of a good fit and ways to diagnose or improve such fit. Following these criticisms, DeCaro and Stokes (2013) analyze institutional fit from behavioral perspective, where they introduce the concept of "social fit". Social fit indicates how well different rules and decision making procedures match with *human expectations* and *local behavioral patterns* (emphasis added) (*ibid.*). Using the principles of human agency and institutional analysis from social psychology, they develop an interdisciplinary framework to address these problems. Through the framework, they investigate social aspect of fit and lay down the concept of institutional acceptance as an indicator of social fit of public participatory programs. They show how social fit contributes to biophysical, political, social, and economic sustainable fit.

Table 6-1: Key concepts of institutional fit

Sl. No.	Concepts	Key features	Authors	Area	Case	Comments
1	Social fit	How well different rules and decision making procedures match with human expectations and local behavioral patterns?	Daniel A. DeCaro and Michael K. Stokes	US	Public participation in Deer and Elk population growth control	Used case studies done by others to demonstrate the framework they developed
2	Contextual fit	How well different rules match with local conditions?	Raul P. Lejano and Savita Shankar	India	Microfinance	It shows how microfinance lending programs evolve as per local context.
3	Spatial fit	How well resource management institutions match with the bio-geophysical properties of the resource they seek to manage?	Oran R. Young	-	Environmental problems and changes	Book
4	Functional fit	How well resource use mechanisms or institutional attributes match with ecosystem functionality, i.e., the ecosystem properties or functions addressed through them?	1. Julia A. Ekstrom and Oran R. Young 2. Graeme S. Cumming, David H. M. Cumming, and Charles L. Redman	1. US 2. Southern Africa and the Southern United States	1. Estuary management 2. Land and water allocation	- -
5	Dynamic fit	The ability to adapt to ecosystem dynamics – Climate change, etc.	Elke Herrfahrdt-Pähle	South Africa	Water Governance	It shows how institutional arrangements deal with faster environmental changes and resource over use.

On these lines, Hiedanpää (2013), using a case of southwestern Finland, evaluates failure of institutional arrangements to improve wolf protection and asserts that both habit breaking and habit taking are the key factors to be considered in attaining fit. He emphasizes on public participation in policy making and their acceptance while focusing on habit taking among rural communities. In addition, recent literature also criticizes institutional blueprints - the 'one size fits all' approach of institutional arrangements applied to a wide range of diverse contexts (Berkes 2007; Ostrom 2008; Lejano and Shankar 2013).

This is mainly because of the failure of these institutional arrangements to match with particular contexts and expectations of local actors. The multidimensional diversity of communities within and across regions/states/ countries brings further complexity to blueprints. Hence, Lejano and Shankar (2013) emphasize on contextual fit of policy design in the specific setting and its link to effective governance. They describe formal institutional arrangements as text and particular place and communities as a context and evaluate match between the two (text and context) using a case of microfinance in India. They also assessed how local actors fitted the available alternative institutional arrangements of microfinance to their individual situations or expectations. Hence, contextualization of institutions (contextual fit) also play an important role for institutions to be effective (Lejano and Shankar 2013). As we can see from this literature review (see Table 6-1 for a survey of the most important concepts), although the role of public participation and contextualization in institutional fit is emphasized, the role of actors' expectations remains unclear. This study makes an attempt to address this issue empirically by narrowing the focus on social fit.

6.2.2 *Institutional Fit in development-induced displacement and rehabilitation*

Since most of the infrastructure development projects are proposed by government authorities, the institutional arrangements for the associated DIDR are also designed and implemented by the same authorities. This top-down perspective currently prevails in most of the policy making context surrounding the DIDR. It is often assumed that the principle of monetary compensation is sufficient to achieve the intended outcome of rehabilitation and since majority of the displaced people do not actively contest this, the institutional arrangements for the DIDR are considered to be 'socially' fit (Cernea 2003).

However, we argue that for the DIDR to achieve its intended outcome, institutional arrangements have to be designed and deployed through a multilateral and participatory approach. Through this, displaced farmers can be actively engaged in the process of design and implementation of the DIDR. Hence, 'institutional acceptance' as an indicator of social fit, assumes great importance (DeCaro and Stokes 2013). Institutional acceptance refers to "the extent to which individuals endorse a set of rights, rules, or decision making procedures" (*p.5*). But this variable only indicates whether actors in a particular socio-ecological system accept or reject particular institutional arrangements. An actor simply accepts something if there is no alternative available for it. To get a clearer perspective on institutional acceptance, there is need to gauge an actor's preference for a set of alternative institutional arrangements. This serves much more an information source of social fit than institutional acceptance in world with no alternatives, and we call it 'institutional preference'. In this study, we therefore analyze the farmers' preferences towards compensation for their land and house acquisition. The results not only explain the role of how institutional preferences in social fit but also explain the driving factors in contextualization of institutional arrangements. The next section explains briefly the empirical method used for data collection and analysis.

6.3 Empirical Approach

6.3.1 Contingent Ranking Experiment

We apply a contingent ranking experimental approach to analyze the farmers' preferences for compensation packages. In this method, the respondents are asked to rank a discrete set of compensation packages from the most to the least preferred. Contingent ranking approach has been widely applied in several areas including economic analysis of forestry, land, water, biodiversity, health, transport, labor and marketing to name a few (Beggs et al. 1981; Garrod and Willis 1997; Foster and Mourato 2000; Hanley et al. 2001; Bateman et al. 2006; González et al. 2009; Kockelman et al. 2012; Veettil et al. 2013). Rankings of alternative compensation packages by the respondents in contingent ranking design is much more informative than mere knowing respondents' most preferred package (Fok et al. 2012; Long and Freese 2014). The first and the foremost step in designing a contingent ranking is to figure out the alternative options comprising relevant attributes with different levels.

In this study, we first identified the attributes and their levels from the literature and past DIDR cases. Some modifications were made after focus group discussion (FGD) and pilot survey in the study area. There are two attributes identified in the context of our study – compensation for land acquisition and compensation for house acquisition (Table 6-2). Three levels are set for the land acquisition compensation attribute namely, cash compensation (*MONEY*), land for land compensation (*LANDFORLAND*) and self-employment training and support (*SELFEMPLY*). For house acquisition compensation, two levels are identified – i) site to construct a house (*SITE*) and ii) constructed house in relocation area (*HOUSE*). Other levels regarding land compensation attributes could be government employment based provisions. However, they are not considered in the experiment as they are practically not viable to implement due to large-scale displacement of farmers and lack of skills required for employment.

Table 6-2: Compensation attributes and their levels in contingent ranking experiment

Attribute	Levels
Compensation for land acquisition	1. Cash compensation (on per acre basis) (MONEY)
	2. Land for land compensation subject to ceiling of two acres and cash compensation for remaining land (LANDFORLAND)
	3. Self-employment training and cash compensation (SELFEMPLY)
Compensation for house acquisition	1. Site and Cash to construct a house that is based on evaluation of the house to be submerged (SITE)
	2. Constructed house based on the size of an original house that is subjected to acquisition/submergence (HOUSE)

Six alternative compensation packages are built based on these attribute levels (Table 6-3). The status quo compensation package, which is currently in practice, comprises *MONEY* and *SITE* (*COMP_PACKAGE_1*). During the experiments, farmers were asked to rank these alternative options of compensation packages on the scale from 1 to 6 with 1 being the most preferred and 6 being the least.

Table 6-3: Illustrative contingent ranking question

Options	Compensation packages	Ranking
1	MONEY + SITE (*COMP_PACKAGE_1*)	☐
2	MONEY + HOUSE (*COMP_PACKAGE_2*)	☐
3	LAND + SITE (*COMP_PACKAGE_3*)	☐
4	LAND + HOUSE (*COMP_PACKAGE_4*)	☐
5	SELF-EMPLOYMENT + SITE (*COMP_PACKAGE_5*)	☐
6	SELF-EMPLOYMENT + HOUSE (*COMP_PACKAGE_6*)	☐

Important respondent-specific variables influencing farmers' preferences are used as interaction terms in the model (Table 6-4). Land holding of the farmer (*LAND_HOLDING*) indicates the wealth of the farmer. The farmers with larger land holding are expected to prefer the cash based compensation package as the most preferred option since that can fetch them large compensation, which can be used to buy another piece of land or be invested in other income generating activities. Respondent's age (*AGE*) could also influence farmers' preferences for compensation. As age of the respondent increases, a land-based compensation package could be more preferred as older farmers are less likely to move to alternative employment. A farmer's preference could also be influenced by the number of households in his family (*NO_OF_HH*). The likelihood of preferring self-employment training is higher in the case of larger households. The primary occupation of the respondent could also influence their preferences (*OCCUPATION*) since non-farmers are less likely to prefer a land-based compensation packages. In addition to these variables, gender (*GENDER*) and farmers' education (*EDUCATION*) could also play a role in their decision (Mahapatra and Mitchell 2001; Deressa et al. 2009). A description of these respondent-specific variables is provided in Table 6-4.

Table 6-4: Description of respondent-specific variables

Sl. No.	Variable name	Description
1	LAND_HOLDING	The respondent's land holding (acres)
2	AGE	Age of the respondent (Years)
3	NO_OF_HH	Number of households
4	OCCUPATION	Main occupation of the respondent; =1 if agriculture and 0 otherwise
5	GENDER	Gender of the respondent; 1 if male and 0 if female
6	EDUCATION	Years of education of the respondent

Based on observation, discussions and survey of previously affected farmers in the study area, we noticed that many farmers who could retain some land after submergence have improved their land (dry land or irrigated land) quality by investing an amount from the received compensation. They however could not buy new land. The main reasons for not buying other land are either high transaction costs, or insufficiency of the compensation amount or unavailability of land in the vicinity. However, rather than buying less land somewhere else, some farmers invested the amount in improving the remaining land in terms of conversion of dry land into irrigation, enhancing fertility by putting a layer of fine black soil from the submerged land or any other infrastructure developments. Thus, farmers' preferences could be influenced by the amount of their land submerged. Hence, two scenarios are designed under which farmers rank the six alternative compensation packages two times – i) if the entire piece of land is acquired/submerged and ii) if a portion of land is acquired. That is, to examine whether farmers' preferences differ under complete land acquisition and under a portion of land acquisition.

6.3.2 Hypothesis and Model Specification

It is hypothesized that, given the alternative choices, farmers would not necessarily prefer monetary compensation strictly over other methods. We test this hypothesis by conducting a contingent ranking experiment and estimating the data using a rank-ordered logit model (ROLM), where dependent variable is ordinal rankings of the options of compensation packages. The *status quo* compensation package, monetary compensation + site for house construction (*COMP_PACKAGE_1*), is kept as a base category. Rank one (1) represents the most preferred compensation package and subsequent rankings represent preferences in descending order. This implies farmers' preferences for compensation packages over the current package in practice (base category). ROLM has the advantage that it takes care of tied ranks as well as when some alternatives are unranked (Fok et al. 2012; Long and Freese 2014). ROLM can take respondent-specific explanatory variables, option-specific explanatory variables or a combination of both (*ibid.*). Hence, ROLM is an appropriate tool to analyze ranked-ordered data. Respondent's rankings are assumed to be sequential and probabilities of subsequent rankings are conditional on the previous rankings.

Let's consider that there are n options, which a respondent i ranks in a sequence. Let $y_r = n$, which indicates that option n is chosen a rank, r (r^{th} preference). That is, y_r takes on integer values from 1 to n, where 1 is the most preferred and n is the least preferred. Here, it is assumed that respondent i has a certain utility U_{in} for each option n. A model for such data takes the form:

$$U_{in} = V_{in} + \epsilon_{in} \tag{1}$$

Here, ϵ_{in} is a random component, and V_{in} is a systematic component that is specified as linear in parameters:

$$V(q_{in}, s_i) = \beta_0 q_{in} + \beta_1 s_i \tag{2}$$

Where, q_{in} is the compensation attribute of option n; and s_i is respondent i's vector of demographic attributes.

Then the probability of the first choice made by the respondent i is $P_i(y_1 = n_1 | X)$. The probability of the second choice is conditional on the first choice[1]. Hence, the probability of the second choice made by the respondent i is $P_i(y_2 = n_2 | X, y_1 = n_1)$. Similarly, the probability of the third choice is given as $P_i(y_3 = n_3 | X, y_1 = n_1, y_2 = n_2)$. The complete data provide a full set of

---

[1] If $y_1 = n_1$, then $y_2 \neq n_1$.

rankings among the *n* options. The probability model based on this data generates the probability of the complete ordering,

$$P_i(U_{i1} > U_{i2} > U_{i3} \ldots \ldots > U_{iN}) = \prod_{n=1}^{N} \left[\frac{\exp(V_{in})}{\sum_{k=n}^{N} \exp(V_{ik})} \right] \tag{3}$$

6.3.3 Sample Data

The primary data from the farmers, who are going to be displaced in the third and final phase of the UKP, was gathered through face-to-face interviews. The interviews were conducted in the Southern Indian state of Karnataka over a period of four months in the year 2012-13. The state has undertaken several irrigation and other development projects, one of which is currently being implemented in its final phase. The author along with three enumerators conducted experiments in four different villages with 50 randomly selected farmers in each village (Table 6-5, see Figure 5-1 on page 73 for location of these villages). The enumerators were specially trained and pilot surveys were conducted before starting the actual interviews. Pilot surveys, involving 10 farmers in nearby selected villages, were undertaken to check the plausibility of the experimental design. Based on responses in pilot survey, some changes were incorporated into the actual contingent ranking experiment.

Table 6-5: Description of the study sample

Sl. No	Village	Sample size
1	Chikka Samshi	50
2	Hire Samshi	50
3	Gaddanakeri	50
4	Govinakoppa	50
	Total	**200**

To make it convenient for both enumerators and respondents during the interview, the questions and basic information about the experiment to the respondents in the questionnaires were written both in English and native Kannada languages. In order to avoid any expectations among the farmers that may result from the experiment, they were provided sufficient information and the experiment was clearly explained at the beginning of experiment (see annexure E for detailed information provided to farmers). Besides that, details of all the compensation packages, their attributes as well as the contingent ranking experiment setting were explained to the farmers. During the interviews, farmers were able to rank the alternative compensation packages. Table 6-6 shows the descriptive statistics of the respondent-specific explanatory variables. Only less than 5 percent of the observations in the sample are female (*GENDER*) and non-agriculture (*OCCUPATION*) as the main occupation respectively, effect of which cannot be observed with these minimal observations. Hence, these two variables - *GENDER* and *OCCUPATION* - are dropped from the analysis.

Table 6-6: Descriptive statistics of respondent-specific variables of sample farmers (N = 2400)

Variable	Mean	Std. Dev.	Min	Max
LAND_HOLDING (Acre)	8.00	6.60	0.3	40
NO_OF_HH	8.13	4.51	2	44
MALE_HH (No. of male households)	4.16	2.72	1	24
AGE (Years)	52.72	12.35	26	86
GENDER (Male = 1, Female = 0)	0.96	0.21	0	1
EDUCATION (Years of schooling)	4.94	1.16	0	15
OCCUPATION (Agriculture =1 and 0 otherwise)	0.96	0.20	0	1

As mentioned earlier each farmer ranks the set of six compensation packages twice (when land under complete and partial submergence scenarios). The dummy is created for this (*LAND_SUB* = 0 if land submerges completely; and = 1 if it submerges partially). In the analysis, each rank represents one observation. Therefore, each farmer generates 12 observations (6 x 2). Hence, rankings of 200 farmers totally generate 2400 observations. The frequency of farmers' ranking of compensation packages is given in appendix (see Table 6-9).

6.4   Description of Results

Using the contingent ranking experiment data about farmers' preferences towards the compensation packages, different ranked order logit models were run to explore the determinants underlying the farmers' preferences. First, we tried the ROLM by including the total number of households (*NO_OF_HH*) with all other variables. The effect of this variable was not significant and thus, dropped from the models. Table 6-7 shows the results of the selected ROLM models. The results are compared between two scenarios – preferences under the complete land submergence (CLS) and preferences under the partial land submergence (PLS). In models 1 and 2 we tested the effect of number of male households (*MALE_HH*) on the decision. This variable also yielded no significant effect on the preferences. Therefore, models 3 and 4 are tested without *MALE_HH* and thus, are considered to be the best fit models. The results of model 3 and 4 represent farmers' preferences under the situations of the CLS and the PLS respectively. The results significantly differ in both the scenarios.

Table 6-7: Estimation results of rank-ordered logit models

Variables	(1 = CLS) PREF_RANK	(2 = PLS) PREF_RANK	(3 = CLS) PREF_RANK	(4 = PLS) PREF_RANK
COMP_PACKAGE_2	-0.115	0.0965	-0.0996	0.0825
	(0.267)	(0.284)	(0.221)	(0.233)
COMP_PACKAGE_3	-0.758***	-0.353	-0.783***	-0.507**
	(0.287)	(0.303)	(0.236)	(0.243)
COMP_PACKAGE_4	-0.590**	-0.137	-0.679***	-0.281
	(0.291)	(0.303)	(0.236)	(0.236)
COMP_PACKAGE_5	0.168	0.359	0.314	0.459*
	(0.297)	(0.305)	(0.243)	(0.246)
COMP_PACKAGE_6	0.716**	0.990***	0.883***	1.066***
	(0.313)	(0.309)	(0.253)	(0.256)
COMP_PACKAGE_2#LAND_HOLDING	0.00692	-0.0232	0.00733	-0.0228
	(0.0175)	(0.0191)	(0.0167)	(0.0184)
COMP_PACKAGE_3#LAND_HOLDING	-0.00679	-0.0275	-0.00657	-0.0312
	(0.0188)	(0.0198)	(0.0181)	(0.0193)
COMP_PACKAGE_4#LAND_HOLDING	-0.00460	-0.0334*	-0.00567	-0.0352*
	(0.0188)	(0.0194)	(0.0182)	(0.0192)
COMP_PACKAGE_5#LAND_HOLDING	-0.0433**	-0.0582***	-0.0398*	-0.0552***
	(0.0210)	(0.0210)	(0.0204)	(0.0206)
COMP_PACKAGE_6#LAND_HOLDING	-0.0675***	-0.0749***	-0.0645***	-0.0712***
	(0.0214)	(0.0212)	(0.0210)	(0.0205)
COMP_PACKAGE_2#EDUCATION	0.00547	-0.00409	0.00495	-0.00403
	(0.0278)	(0.0279)	(0.0276)	(0.0278)
COMP_PACKAGE_3#EDUCATION	0.0382	0.0211	0.0383	0.0243
	(0.0285)	(0.0296)	(0.0282)	(0.0294)
COMP_PACKAGE_4#EDUCATION	0.0582**	0.0271	0.0594**	0.0281
	(0.0288)	(0.0292)	(0.0286)	(0.0291)
COMP_PACKAGE_5#EDUCATION	-0.0518*	-0.0510*	-0.0542*	-0.0532*
	(0.0298)	(0.0298)	(0.0296)	(0.0297)
COMP_PACKAGE_6#EDUCATION	-0.0484	-0.0505	-0.0511*	-0.0535*
	(0.0301)	(0.0310)	(0.0298)	(0.0307)
COMP_PACKAGE_2#MALE_HH	0.00415	-0.00290		
	(0.0422)	(0.0447)		
COMP_PACKAGE_3#MALE_HH	-0.00620	-0.0411		
	(0.0441)	(0.0480)		

Table 6-7 continued

Variables	(1 = CLS) PREF_RA NK	(2 = PLS) PREF_RA NK	(3 = CLS) PREF_RA NK	(4 = PLS) PREF_RAN K
COMP_PACKAGE_4#MALE_HH	-0.0224	-0.0376		
	(0.0450)	(0.0491)		
COMP_PACKAGE_5#MALE_HH	0.0392	0.0270		
	(0.0460)	(0.0475)		
COMP_PACKAGE_6#MALE_HH	0.0427	0.0212		
	(0.0471)	(0.0456)		
Observations	1,200	1,200	1,200	1,200
Number of groups	200	200	200	200
Psuedo R-squared	0.0348	0.0332	0.0340	0.0320
Log likelihood	-1244	-1238	-1245	-1239
Chi-sqaured	89.71	84.89	87.55	81.83
p-value	8.32e-11	5.72e-10	0	0

Note: Standard errors in parentheses; *** p<0.01, ** p<0.05, * p<0.1; CLS and PLS are complete and partial
    land submergence situations respectively.

In case of the CLS scenario, land with site/house based and employment with house based compensation packages are significant. The variable, *LAND_HOLDING* significantly influenced the farmers' preferences towards *COMP_PACKAGE_5*, and *COMP_PACKAGE_6* as their most preferred compensation packages vis-à-vis existing package. *OCCUPATION* influenced the farmers' preferences towards *COMP_PACKAGE_4*, *COMP_PACKAGE_5*, and *COMP_PACKAGE_6* as their most preferred compensation packages ahead of *COMP_PACKAGE_1*.

Whereas, in case of the PLS, land with site based and employment with site/house based compensation packages are significant. *LAND_HOLDING* significantly influenced the farmers' preferences towards *COMP_PACKAGE_4*, *COMP_PACKAGE_5*, and *COMP_PACKAGE_6* as their most preferred compensation packages. *EDUCATION* influenced the farmers' preferences towards *COMP_PACKAGE_5*, and *COMP_PACKAGE_6* as their most preferred compensation packages vis-à-vis *COMP_PACKAGE_1*.

Unlike linear regression models, the ROLM results do not offer a direct meaningful interpretation of the coefficients (Long and Freese 2014). Therefore, the coefficients are transformed (exponentiated) and interpreted as odds ratios. This transformation is done through the formula: $(= 100\{exp(coeff.value) - 1\})$. The transformed coefficient value - in case of continuous variables - explains percentage change in the odds of ranking particular compensation package ahead of base-category compensation package for a unit change in an explanatory variable, keeping other variables constant. Whereas, in case of categorical variable, transformed coefficient value explains percentage change in the odds of ranking particular compensation package ahead of base-category compensation package for variable changing from base category to other category, all else being equal. Table 6-8 shows transformed coefficients of explanatory variables.

In case of the CLS scenario, an acre increase in land holding decreases the odds of ranking *COMP_PACKAGE_5* and *COMP_PACKAGE_6* ahead of base-category compensation package (*COMP_PACKAGE_1*) by 4% and 6% respectively, holding other variables constant. As years of schooling increases, the odds of ranking *COMP_PACKAGE_4* ahead of *COMP_PACKAGE_1* increases by 6%, whereas, the odds of ranking *COMP_PACKAGE_5* and *COMP_PACKAGE_6* ahead *COMP_PACKAGE_1* decreases by 5%. Whereas, in case of PLS scenario, an acre increase in land holding decreases the odds of ranking *COMP_PACKAGE_4, COMP_PACKAGE_5* and *COMP_PACKAGE_6* ahead of *COMP_PACKAGE_1* by 3.5%, 5% and 7% respectively, holding other variables constant. As years of schooling increases, the odds of ranking *COMP_PACKAGE_5* and *COMP_PACKAGE_6* ahead of *COMP_PACKAGE_1* decreases by 5%. In general, *LAND_HOLDING* and *OCCUPATION* variables have the negative influence on the odds of ranking to land based and employment based compensation packages ahead of status quo compensation package.

Table 6-8: Exponentiated coefficients of rank-ordered logit models

Variables	CLS	PLS
COMP_PACKAGE_2	-9.48	8.60
COMP_PACKAGE_3	-54.30***	-39.77**
COMP_PACKAGE_4	-49.29***	-24.50
COMP_PACKAGE_5	36.89	58.25*
COMP_PACKAGE_6	141.81***	190.37***
COMP_PACKAGE_2#LAND_HOLDING	0.74	-2.25
COMP_PACKAGE_3#LAND_HOLDING	-0.65	-3.07
COMP_PACKAGE_4#LAND_HOLDING	-0.57	-3.46*
COMP_PACKAGE_5#LAND_HOLDING	-3.90*	-5.37***
COMP_PACKAGE_6#LAND_HOLDING	-6.25***	-6.87***

Table 6-8 continued

Variables	CLS	PLS
COMP_PACKAGE_2#EDUCATION	0.50	-0.40
COMP_PACKAGE_3#EDUCATION	3.90	2.46
COMP_PACKAGE_4#EDUCATION	6.12**	2.85
COMP_PACKAGE_5#EDUCATION	-5.28*	-5.18*
COMP_PACKAGE_6#EDUCATION	-4.98*	-5.21*

Note: *** $p<0.01$, ** $p<0.05$, * $p<0.1$; CLS and PLS are complete and partial land submergence situations respectively.

6.5 Discussion

We used a choice modelling approach to estimate the trade-offs between different compensation attributes of land and house acquisition provided in the form of alternative compensation packages. The survey is conducted using contingent ranking approach, in which respondents are asked to rank a set of six alternative compensation packages from the most preferred as rank 1 to the least preferred as rank 6. In order to make the farmers better understand and visualize the choices, visual aids in the form of color pictures representing the attributes of different compensation packages are used during the contingent ranking experiment. As discussed in the above section, the coefficients of explanatory variables are estimated using the ROLM (Rank-ordered Logit Model).

Results in both the cases indicate that compensation packages having land and employment training options are significantly preferred by the farmers over monetary compensation. Farmers with a smaller land holding and lesser education are more likely to prefer land-based and employment-based compensation packages as their most preferred compensation packages over the *status quo* of money-based compensation package. This is because farmers with a small land holding and less education lack the information about land transactions, the networks, and the ability either to repurchase a land or to regenerate income through other means. Thus, they prefer employment-based or land-based compensation package for their further income generation. However, farmers with a larger land holding and higher education are less likely to prefer land-based and employment based compensation packages over *status quo* compensation package. This is because land holding is the manifestation of wealth of the farmers and education implies learning, information processing and acquiring ability, which brings an ability to repurchase land either fully or partly or to generate income by other means of their own.

However, in case of the CLS, education positively influences the odds of ranking land based compensation packages (*COMP_PACKAGE_4*) ahead of *status quo* compensation package (money + site). This is because education brings awareness that repurchasing the land in the region is very difficult and complete land submergence may end up being landless in the future. Hence, getting at least a minimum of land from the government will secure them from being landless and enable continue agriculture as a part of their income generating activity. These results validate our hypothesis that the farmers, given the options, prefer compensation packages containing land-based and employment-based options. Therefore, rather than estimating only the most preferred compensation package or understanding mere acceptance or rejection of a particular compensation package, examining farmers' preferences for a range of compensation packages generated more information. In addition, their links with farmers' characteristics are identified, which implies which type of farmers prefers what and why. Such an understanding facilitates in achieving a better institutional fit of the DIDR. Hence, institutional preference as an indicator of social fit plays a significant role if public participation is to be taken into account while forming or modifying institutions of the DIDR.

6.6 Conclusion

In this paper, we have examined the farmers' preferences towards compensation for the DIDR. This is among the first studies to examine preference as an indicator of social fit. We do this for the case of public participation component of the DIDR. The contemporary institutional arrangements of the DIDR are criticized for their lack of not involving those who are to be displaced by development projects. Hence, a more intense analysis of farmers' preferences regarding the choice of compensation modes is definitely much necessitated. In order to examine the farmers' preferences towards compensation packages, we employed a contingent ranking experimental approach and used a rank-ordered logit model on a primary dataset of 200 farmers.

The findings of this study assert that the preferences towards compensation packages are significantly different from the *status quo* compensation package – monetary-based compensation for land and house acquisition. This implies that farmers' expectations differ from the compensation provisions of contemporary institutional arrangements of the DIDR. Land holding and education of the farmers influence their preferences for different compensation packages. Farmers with large land holding are less likely to prefer compensation packages other than the *status quo* as their most preferred packages. Conversely, the farmers with a small land holding are more likely to prefer a land-based and employment-based compensation package as their most preferred packages to the *status quo*. In addition, the farmers' preferences differ under the CLS and the PLS scenarios. In case of the CLS, educated farmers are more likely to prefer a land-based compensation package as their most preferred option. Besides this, the influence of education on the farmers' preferences towards land-based and employment-based compensation packages is negative in both the CLS and the PLS scenarios.

Therefore, the farmers, given the alternative options, prefer land- and employment-based compensation packages ahead of the *status quo* compensation package. This information about preferences in both the scenarios plays an important role if at all the public participation is to be taken into account in achieving a better institutional fit of the DIDR. This in turn implies the need for contextualization of the institutions of the DIDR according to the farmers' expectations and local conditions.

Appendix of Chapter 6

Frequencies of the farmers' rankings of compensation packages is shown in Table 6-9.

Table 6-9: Frequencies of farmers' rankings of compensation packages

Ranking option	Farmers' ranking							
	0	1	2	3	4	5	6	Total
COMP_PACKAGE_1	6	66	36	49	194	24	25	400
COMP_PACKAGE_2	10	36	60	144	57	48	45	400
COMP_PACKAGE_3	10	19	87	45	52	70	117	400
COMP_PACKAGE_4	12	54	45	79	34	99	77	400
COMP_PACKAGE_5	12	46	115	49	25	70	83	400
COMP_PACKAGE_6	12	173	45	22	28	77	43	400
Total	**62**	**394**	**388**	**388**	**390**	**388**	**390**	**2400**

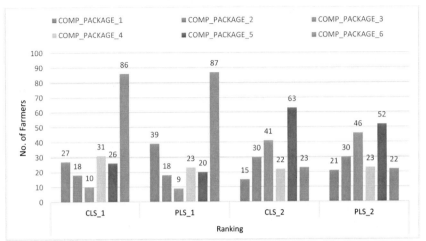

Figure 6-1: Top-two ranked categories under complete land submergence and partial land submergence situations

Note: CLS_1 and PLS_1 represent rank 1 in complete and partial land submergence situations respectively. Similarly, CLS_2 and PLS_2 represent rank 2.

The majority of the farmers chose COMP_PACKAGE_6 as their most preferred package under both the complete (CLS_1) (86) and the partial land submergence (PLS_1) (87) situations (Figure 6-1). The majority of the farmers chose COMP_PACKAGE_5 as their second most preferred package under both the complete (CLS_1) (63) and the partial land submergence (PLS_1) (52) situations, which is followed by COMP_PACKAGE_3.

7 Conclusions, Policy Insights, and Research Scope

Synopsis of Research Findings

The intended outcome for the people displaced due to development projects in India is to resettle them in non-affected areas and to rehabilitate them economically, physically, and socio-culturally. In order to achieve this and minimize the negative effects on the people, institutional arrangements of rehabilitation have been designed and modified several times over a period of five decades. These institutional arrangements are organized as hybrids where land is acquired through top-down approach of monetary compensation principle and displaced people have to re-organize their income activities through a market approach. This thesis shows that institutions do matter in achieving the desired outcome. By investigating three key elements of institutional analysis – organizing modes, institutions of rehabilitation, and characteristics of actors (displaced people) - it is found that the displaced people bear high transaction costs in the current set-up. It is also argued that in addition to allocated property rights, benefits actually depend on 'access' to those rights. Further, it is shown that farmers' preference for different compensation packages as an indicator of social fit plays an important role in contextualizing the institutional arrangement of rehabilitation.

7.1 Summary

The thesis started with explaining the importance of land as a scarce resource for development projects and the consequences of involuntary land acquisition from private land holders, especially in developing countries. The broad issue of land acquisition in development projects is displacement of private land holders, which bears the high risk of causing economic, physical, and socio-cultural disruptions. This poses major challenges in institutionalizing the Development-induced Displacement and Rehabilitation (DIDR) of farmers. India, with high population and fragmented land holdings, is no exception to such the challenges. Hence, displacement and resettlement of farmers in development projects is one of the major contentious issues in economic development of India. After independence in 1947, massive development projects mushroomed throughout India in order to cope with demands of growing population and modernization. Using one such project (Upper Krishna Project (UKP)), the thesis has made an investigation to answer some important questions raised around the issue of the DIDR. The intended aim of the DIDR is effective rehabilitation of the people from an economical, physical, and socio-cultural perspective. As discussed elsewhere (Sections 1.3 and 1.4), although there is some improvement in the rehabilitation procedure and its outcome, they are not up to the expectations of economists, policy makers, external funding agencies and other experts.

Therefore, the main question investigated here is: why did the contemporary institutional arrangements of the DIDR fail to achieve its intended outcomes of rehabilitation and to curb marginalization of displaced people? The key insight from the present analysis is that the contemporary DIDR program somewhat overlooked the core element of economic rehabilitation, that is, regenerating income activities of the displaced people. The entire focus was confined to monetary compensation and to some extent physical and socio-cultural rehabilitation, which are not sufficient for rehabilitation to be effective. The thesis has shown that one important reason for this flawed program was lack of attention to the analysis of land acquisition, and the rehabilitation and resettlement (R&R) concept of development projects from the perspective of institutional economics. Without an understanding of what do the current institutional arrangements of the DIDR contain, how they are reformed, and how they are implemented, an investigation of the R&R issues from the perspective of conventional economics could yield fallacious results. Hence, such an understanding serves as a basis for empirical investigation.

In Chapter 2, details about the institutional reform process of the DIDR and its implementation process were presented. Even after six decades of India's independence, compensation component of the LAA 1894 was the only basis for the DIDR of displaced people. As large developments projects mushroomed throughout India in order to match the pace of growing population and modernization, the DIDR domain of these projects started gaining importance, partly due to heightened public demand for effective R&R. In pursuance of this, the government of India every now and then initiated reforms. Apart from that, individual projects adopted these nationwide institutions with slight modifications according to circumstances. This chapter highlighted that the monetary compensation principle is not sufficient for efficient rehabilitation. In spite of such reforms, the majority of development projects failed to rehabilitate displaced people, who eventually became marginalized and/or even landless after the involuntary displacement. Recently, new institutional arrangements of the DIDR have been proposed, namely "the Right to Fair Compensation and Transparency in Land Acquisition, Rehabilitation, and Resettlement (Amendment) Ordinance 2015." This bill is still under discussion and to be enacted yet but lays down the insights for empirical investigations presented in Chapters 4, 5 and 6.

Before proceeding to the empirical analysis, theoretical foundations for the analysis were laid down in Chapter 3. The DIDR programs of land acquisition in most countries are grounded on a neoclassical approach, where only economic forces are taken into account. However, in addition to these economic forces, rehabilitation of displaced farmers is also influenced by institutions and governance structures. To achieve coherence and depth, the analysis is placed under IoS framework developed by Hagedorn (2008). The IoS framework comprises of four main elements – institutions, governance structures, characteristics of actors and properties of transactions. The IoS framework facilitates to unpack and analyze complex interrelated factors involved in resource (land) management-related issues like the R&R of farmers. First, a comparative analysis of governance structures is done based on transaction cost reasoning. Secondly, the thesis, using the access based-property rights approach, investigates the contemporary institutional arrangements of the DIDR and its implications for farmers' decision to claim compensation. Finally, as farmers' characteristics and their expectations play an important in rehabilitation process, the concept of fit is used to analyze the farmers' preferences towards the DIDR provisions. Taking the IoS framework as a starting point, these three different approaches of New Institutional Economics are adopted to unpack the rehabilitation problems.

In Chapter 4, the question of why the aim of rehabilitating the displaced farmers has not been achieved in the contemporary mode of the DIDR was examined through transaction cost reasoning. To do this, attributes of land purchase transactions under the contemporary R&R framework are analyzed using the lens of Transaction Cost Economics (TCE) and compared with newly proposed mode of governing the R&R. This comparison is made to gauge whether it minimizes the burden of transaction costs on farmers. The guiding principle of TCE is based on efficiency criteria for managing transactions through alternative governance structures. This is achieved by applying the discriminating alignment hypothesis which enables economizing on transaction costs. The core context of contemporary mode of organizing the R&R is based on a hybrid mode, where land is acquired through a top-down approach of monetary compensation principle and the farmers have to re-organize their income activities through a market approach. Whereas in the case of the newly proposed mode, the government internalizes a portion of income re-organization by means of provision of land compensation. For the remaining portion, the farmers get monetary compensation. In addition, there is a compulsory provision of employment to at least one member of each family in the new mode. This analysis revealed the reasons for failure of the contemporary mode of rehabilitation to achieve the desired outcome. The reasons are *ex-post* displacement hazards and associated high transaction costs due to uncertainties in the contemporary mode, which confined the farmers from re-organizing their income generating activities. Whereas in the case of the newly proposed mode of rehabilitation, these effects are partly taken care of by the government. Hence, the contemporary mode is comparatively more inefficient than the newly proposed. The later intends to address these *ex-post* transaction costs by land for land provisions but the impact of innovation can only be assessed in the future.

In Chapter 5, an empirical investigation of institutional arrangements under the contemporary mode of the DIDR is made from the perspective of farmers' access to them, where it is shown that a lack of access to *de jure* property rights produces less than desirable outcomes in the R&R of displaced farmers. A right is accompanied by rules that specify choices a right holder may, must or must not make in order to exercise it. The right to claim compensation of land acquisition is implemented by rules, which specify two methods of claim – the consent method and the arbitration method. The question here is: does a choice between these affect the benefit stream, and if yes, then what factors influence the choice of these awards? Previous literature empirically showed that there is an incentive to claim higher compensation via the arbitration method. Still, many displaced farmers opt for the consent method. Some literature also asserts that wealth in terms of asset holding is the main determinant of the choice of arbitration method. However, in this chapter, it was argued that not only the wealth of farmers but also other factors of 'access' influence farmers' decision in choosing the methods of compensation claim. Using a binary response model on a primary dataset of 200 displaced farmers from the Upper Krishna Irrigation Project, India, the 'access based' hypotheses on the choice of compensation was tested that whether in addition to allocated property rights, benefits actually depend on 'access' to those rights. The results confirmed the role of access to political bargaining power and information in these choice decisions of the displaced farmers. Therefore, farmers lacking access to these end up with less compensation, and this explains their further marginalization despite the presence of a policy framework aimed at their rehabilitation.

Thus, as elicited in Chapters 4 and 5, the reasons for failure of effective R&R under current mode are multifaceted. Apart from this, the researchers have also highlighted the lack of farmer participation during the policy formation stage. There is some literature on 'institutional acceptance' as an indicator of social fit of public participatory programs. However, this variable only indicates whether actors in a particular socio-ecological system accept or reject particular institutional arrangements, which do not acquire other information from the actors. Actors simply accept if there is no alternative available for it. In Chapter 6, therefore, it is shown that 'institutional preference' for compensation is a much better source of information for social fit than institutional acceptance. Hence, institutional preference plays an important role in contextualizing the institutional arrangements of the DIDR. By means of the contingent ranking method, the farmers' preferences towards compensation for their land and house acquisition was examined. In the context of the top-down perspective of involuntary land acquisition and compensation provision, this information of institutional preference explains the driving factors in contextualization of institutional arrangements.

These two appropriately designed and elaborated empirical analyses (Chapter 5 and 6) have shown the importance of institutions in the world of complex economic activities for desirable outcomes. The case of already displaced farmers in the irrigation development project has shown that farmers' lack of having *access mechanisms* impede them from choosing the general award in spite of an incentive of higher compensation claim. This could lead to further marginalization. Whereas, the case of the farmers who are going to be displaced due to a development project to be implemented in the near future has shown the mismatch

between the current institutional arrangements of the DIDR and the farmers expectations. Both cases have revealed the social/contextual misfit of the contemporary institutional arrangements. The overall outcome from the institutional analysis of the R&R of development projects is that institutions matter but need to be contextualized. Therefore, such arrangements may fail to achieve the desirable outcomes unless they are contextualized to the local situation and farmers' expectations are taken care of.

7.2 Policy Insights

A broad policy implication which derives from this analysis is that the focus of the institutional reform process of rehabilitation should be on income generating activities (economic rehabilitation) and not restricted to monetary compensation provisions. Income generating activities should aim towards employment generation through self-employment, small-scale business or by the establishment of agro-based industries in the locality based on the local conditions. In order for these employment generations to be materialized, the institutional arrangements of the DIDR should focus on the development of self-employment skills, portfolio management skills, and small-scale business skills among the displaced farmers and education for household members. In addition, they should also focus on creating environment for establishment of agro-based industries, which create employment for the farmers. For effective public participation, the government should understand the preferences of the farmers who are going to be displaced and consider them in the institutional design process. This will facilitate in designing a relatively fit institutional arrangement of the DIDR that influences the standard of living of the displaced farmers, particularly small farmers.

Both the contemporary mode and the newly proposed mode of organizing the DIDR yield transaction costs to both the farmers and the government. Hence, another way for efficient economic rehabilitation of the displaced farmers is through long-term land lease contracts between the farmers and the government (see Chapter 4). In this way, farmers' income will be sustainable and secured as they get a certain amount of rent as an income seasonally or annually. This approach is better off from the point of view of both farmers and the government. On the one hand, this will be efficient in rehabilitating the farmers. On the other, this will reduce transaction cost as well as the high initial investment burden of rehabilitation on government. This form of organization enables to spread the high initial investment burden over a long term. The long-term lease contract also retains the entitlement of land with farmers, which ensures them the legal rights to grow at least a single crop when water drained out during summer in case of irrigation projects. They will also have the right to borrow credit, get electricity connection, and other rights to grow and protect their crops, which farmers are deprived off in the current and the newly drafted form. Even if they are not able to grow the crop, they get assured a fixed rent for their leased out land from the government. This process will rehabilitate farmers efficiently as transaction costs of both government and farmers will be lower here.

7.3 Research Scope

The thesis made an attempt in scientific enquiry into the issues related to economic governance of rehabilitation and resettlement from the perspective of institutional analysis. It has contributed to the growing body of literature that could create further debates around this line of thought. As enquiry is a continuous process, its gaps give a space for further research. Based on the investigations of modes of governing the DIDR components and their insights, this study proposed an alternative mode, long-term land lease contract. However, this policy implication demands further research on organizing the lease contracts in terms of the lease amount to be decided, lease period, generating information, possible safeguards against post-contract hazards and other terms of contracts. The study also investigates institutional preferences as an indicator of social fit. However, further extensive research in this line will help bring insights for designing or modifying institutions for different scenarios (the complete land submergence (CLS) and the partial land submergence (PLS)) according to the characteristics of the farmers. This study limits its analysis to farmers' decision making regarding the choice compensation claim, governance processes and issues of land purchase transactions, and farmers' preferences. Analyzing other associated factors like corruption and farmers' adaptations to the post-displacement current scenario has potential to yield further and a deeper understanding on the R&R governance issues. However, this thesis attempted to produce relevant insights that may serve as a way towards research in that direction and assist in curbing marginalization of displaced farmers.

References

Alchian, A.A., Demsetz, H. (1973). The Property Right Paradigm. *The Journal of Economic History* 33, 16-27.

Ali, J., Kumar, S. (2011). Information and Communication Technologies (ICTs) and Farmers' Decision-making Across the Agricultural Supply Chain. *International Journal of Information Management* 31, 149-59.

Anonymous (2015). Stamp Duty in India, http://www.stampdutyinindia.com/.

Asif, M. (1999). Land Acquisition Act: Need for an Alternative Paradigm. *Economic and Political Weekly* 34, 1564-6.

Authority, N.C. (2015). Resettlement and Rehabilitation, Online.

Bagchi, K. (2012). The Land Acquisition Debate: A Review. Observer Research Foundation

Bank, A.D. (2007). Compensation and Valuation in Resettlement: Cambodia, People's Republic of China, and India. Rural Development Institute, http://www.adb.org/.

Bank, W. (2014). Average Precipitation in Depth (mm per year)

Barzel, Y. (1997). *Economic Analysis of Property Rights*. Cambridge University Press.

Bateman, I.J., Cole, M., Georgiou, S., Hadley, D. (2006). Comparing Contingent Valuation and Contingent Ranking: A Case Study Considering the Benefits of Urban River Water Quality Improvements. *Journal of Environmental Management* 79, 221-31.

Beggs, S., Cardell, S., Hausman, J. (1981). Assessing the Potential Demand for Electric Cars. *Journal of Eonometrics* 17, 1-19.

Bell, A., Parchomovsky, G. (2001). Takings Reassessed. *Virginia Law Review* 87, 277.

Berkes, F. (2007). Community-based Conservation in a Globalized World. *Proceedings of the National Academy of Sciences* 104, 15188-93.

Berry, S. (1989). Social Institutions and Access to Resources. *Africa* 59, 41-55.

Bogale, A., Korf, B. (2007). To Share or not to Share? (Non-) Violence, Scarcity and Resource Access in Somali Region, Ethiopia. *Journal of Development Studies* 43, 743-65.

Bose, P. (2013). A Land Acquisition Bill with Many Faultlines. *Economic and Political Weekly* 48.

Bromley, D.W. (1991). *Environment and Economy: Property Rights and Public Policy*. Basil Blackwell Ltd.

Bromley, D.W. (2012). Environmental Governance as Stochastic Belief Updating: Crafting Rules to Live by. *Ecology and Society* 17, 14.

Cernea, M.M. (1990). Internal Refugee Flows and Development-induced Population Displacement. *Journal of Refugee Studies* 3, 320-39.

Cernea, M.M. (1997). The Risks and Reconstruction Model for Resettling Displaced Populations. *World Development* 25, 1569-87.

Cernea, M.M. (1998). Impoverishtnent or Social Justice? A Model for Planning Resettlement. *Oxford, New Delhi*.

Cernea, M.M. (2003). For a New Economics of Resettlement: A Sociological Critique of the Compensation Principle. *International Social Science Journal* 55, 37-45.

Cernea, M.M. (2004). Impoverishment Risks, Risk Management, and Reconstruction: A Model of Population Displacement and Resettlement, *UN Symposium on Hydropower and Sustainable Development, Beijing (27–29 October)*.

Cernea, M.M. (2006). Resettlement Management: Denying or Confronting Risks, in: Mathur, H.M. (Ed.), *Managing Resttlement in India: Approaches, Issues, Experiences*. Oxford University Press, New Delhi, India, pp. 19-44.

Chan, N. (2003). Land Acquisition Compensation in China–problems and Answers. *International Real Estate Review* 6, 136-52.

Choudhury, C. (2013). Adivasis and the New Land Acquisition Act, *Economic and Political Weekly*, 12.10.2013 ed.

Cole, D.H. (2010). New Forms of Private Property: Property Rights in Environmental Goods, in: Bouckaert, B. (Ed.), *Property Law and Economics*, 2 ed. Edward Elgar Publishing, Inc. , Massachusetts, USA, p. 225.

Cole, D.H., Grossman, P.Z. (2002). The Meaning of Property Rights: Law versus Economics? *Land Economics* 78, 317-30.

Committee, U.D. (2004). 40 Years of Upper Krishna Project. Krishna Bhagya Jala Nigam Limited, Bangalore, India, pp. 1-321.

Cox, M. (2012). Diagnosing Institutional Fit: A Formal Perspective. *Ecology and Society* 17, 54.

Das, S. (2006). The Land Acquisition Laws in India: An Overview with Some Suggestions for Amendment, in: Mathur, H.M. (Ed.), *Managing Resettlement in India: Approaches, Issues, Experiences*. Oxford University Press, New Delhi, India, pp. 137-72.

Dash, S.P. (2009). Displacement and Resettlement Management in Thailand. *Economic and Political Weekly* 44, 23-6.

De Wet, C. (2001). Economic development and population displacement: Can everybody win? *Economic and Political Weekly*, 4637-46.

De Wet, C. (2006a). Risk, Complexity and Local Initiative in Forced Resettlement Outcomes, in: De Wet, C. (Ed.), *Development-induced Displacement: Problems, Policies, and People*. Berghahn Books.

De Wet, C.J. (2006b). *Development-induced Displacement: Problems, Policies, and People*. Berghahn Books.

Debnath, B. (2008). Land Acquisition and National Highways. *Economic and Political Weekly* 43, 4-74.

DeCaro, D.A., Stokes, M.K. (2013). Public Participation and Institutional Fit: A Social– psychological Perspective. *Ecology and Society* 18, 40.

Deneke, T.T., Mapedza, E., Amede, T. (2011). Institutional Implications of Governance of Local Common Pool Resources on Livestock Water Productivity in Ethiopia. *Experimental Agriculture* 47, 99-111.

Deressa, T.T., Hassan, R.M., Ringler, C., Alemu, T., Yesuf, M. (2009). Determinants of Farmers' Choice of Adaptation Methods to Climate Change in the Nile Basin of Ethiopia. *Global Environmental Change* 19, 248-55.

Desai, K., Jain, V., Pandey, R., Srikant, P., Trivedi, U. (2007). Rehabilitation of the Indira Sagar Pariyojana Displaced. *Economic and Political Weekly* 42, 27-36.

Desai, M. (2011). Land Acquisition Law and the Proposed Changes. *Economic and Political Weekly* 46, 95-100.

Development, M.o.R. (1996). Draft National Policy for Rehabilitation of Persons-Displaced as a Consequence of Acquisition of Land. *Economic and Political Weekly* 31, 1541-5.

Development, S.C.o.R. (2012). The Land Acquisition, Rehabilitation and Resettlement Bill, 2011, in: Resources, D.o.L. (Ed.). Lok Sabha Secretariat, New Delhi, pp. 1-318.

Doremus, H. (2003). Takings and Transitions. *Journal of Land Use & Environmental Law* 19, 1-46.

Editorials, E. (2011). Modifying the Terms of Compensation. *Economic and Political Weekly* 46, 9.

Edwards-Jones, G. (2006). Modelling Farmer Decision-making: Concepts, Pogress and Challenges. *Animal Science* 82, 783-90.

Ekstrom, J.A., Young, O.R. (2009). Evaluating Functional Fit between a Set of Institutions and an Ecosystem. *Ecology and Society* 14, 16.

Epstein, R.A. (2012). Physical and Regulatory Takings: One Distinction Too Many. *Stanford Law Review Online* 64, 99.

Feder, G., Feeny, D. (1991). Land Tenure and Property Rights: Theory and Implications for Development Policy. *The World Bank Economic Review* 5, 135-53.

Fernandes, W. (1998). Land Acquisition (Amendment) Bill, 1998-Rights of Project-Affected People Ignored. *Economic and Political Weekly* 33, 2703-6.

Fischel, W.A., Shapiro, P. (1989). A Constitutional Choice Model of Compensation for Takings. *International Review of Law and Economics* 9, 115-28.

Fok, D., Paap, R., Van Dijk, B. (2012). A Rank-Ordered Logit Model with Unobserved Heterogeneity in Ranking Capabilities. *Journal of Applied Econometrics* 27, 831-46.

Folke, C., Pritchard, L., Berkes, F., Colding, J., Svedin, U. (2007). The Problem of Fit between Ecosystems and Institutions: Ten Years Later. *Ecology and Society* 12, 30.

Foster, V., Mourato, S. (2000). Valuing the Multiple Impacts of Pesticide Use in the UK: A Contingent Ranking Approach. *Journal of Agricultural Economics* 51, 1-21.

Franco, J.C. (2008). Making Land Rights Accessible: Social Movements and Political-legal Innovation in the Rural Philippines. *The Journal of Development Studies* 44, 991-1022.

Furubotn, E.G., Richter, R. (2005). *Institutions and Economic Theory: The Contribution of the New Institutional Economics*. University of Michigan Press.

Garikipati, S. (2005). Consulting the Development-Displaced Regarding their Resettlement: Is there a Way? *Journal of Refugee Studies* 18, 340-61.

Garrod, G.D., Willis, K.G. (1997). The Non-use Benefits of Enhancing Forest Biodiversity: A Contingent Ranking Study. *Ecological Economics* 21, 45-61.

Gatzweiler, F.W., Hagedorn, K. (2002). The evolution of institutions in transition. *International Journal of Agricultural Resources, Governance and Ecology* 2, 37-58.

González, C., Johnson, N., Qaim, M. (2009). Consumer Acceptance of Second Generation GM Foods: The Case of Biofortified Cassava in the North-east of Brazil. *Journal of Agricultural Economics* 60, 604-24.

Gulati, A., Meinzen-Dick, R.S., Raju, K.V. (2005). *Institutional Reforms in Indian Irrigation*. Sage, New Delhi.

Hagedorn, K. (2008). Particular requirements for institutional analysis in nature-related sectors. *European Review of Agricultural Economics* 35, 357-84.

Hagedorn, K. (2015). Can the Concept of Integrative and Segregative Institutions Contribute to the Framing of Institutions of Sustainability? *Sustainability* 7, 584-611.

Haller, T., Fokou, G., Mbeyale, G., Meroka, P. (2013). How Fit Turns into Misfit and Back: Institutional Transformations of Pastoral Commons in African Floodplains. *Ecology and Society* 18, 34.

Hanley, N., Mourato, S., Wright, R.E. (2001). Choice Modelling Approaches: A Superior Alternative for Environmental Valuatioin? *Journal of Economic Surveys* 15, 435-62.

Herrfahrdt-Pähle, E. (2010). Applying the Concept of Fit to Water Governance Reforms in South Africa. *Ecology and Society* 19, 25.

Hiedanpää, J. (2013). Institutional Misfits: Law and Habits in Finnish Wolf Policy. *Ecology and Society* 18, 24.

Huffman, W.E. (1974). Decision Making: The Role of Education. *American Journal of Agricultural Economics* 56, 85-97.

India, C.O.o. (2011a). Bagalkot District : Census 2011 data.

India, G.o. (1894). The Land Acquisition Act 1894, in: Resources, D.o.L. (Ed.), http://megrevenuedm.gov.in/acts/land-aquisition-act-1894.pdf, p. 27.

India, G.o. (1964). The Constitution (Seventeeth Amendment) Act 1964, in: India, C.o. (Ed.), http://www.archive.india.gov.in/govt/documents/amendment/amend17.htm.

India, G.o. (1984). The Land Acquisition Act, 1894 in: Development, M.o.R. (Ed.).

India, G.o. (2004). National Policy on Resettlement and Rehabilitation 2004, in: Development, M.o.R. (Ed.).

India, G.o. (2006). National Rehabilitation Policy 2006, in: Development, M.o.R. (Ed.), http://dolr.nic.in/dolr/downloads/pdfs/NRP2006-draft.pdf.

India, G.o. (2007a). Minor Irrigation Census (2006-07): Concepts and Definitions in: Resources, M.o.W. (Ed.), http://micensus.gov.in/.

India, G.o. (2007b). National Rehabilitation and Resettlement Policy 2007, in: Development, M.o.R. (Ed.), http://dolr.nic.in/dolr/downloads/pdfs/NRRP2007.pdf.

India, G.o. (2009). National Register of Large Dams Report. Central Water Cimmission (CWC), http://www.cwc.gov.in/CWC%20Citizen%20Charter.pdf.

India, G.o. (2011b). Economic Activity, in: Ministry of Home Affairs, I. (Ed.). Office of the Registrar   General   and   Census   Commissioner, http://censusindia.gov.in/Census_And_You/economic_activity.aspx.

India, G.o. (2011c). The Land Acquisition, Rehabilitation and Resettlement (LARR) Bill, 2011,   in: Resources,   D.o.L.   (Ed.), http://rural.nic.in/sites/downloads/general/ls%20version%20of%20larr%20%20bill.p df.

India, G.o. (2011d). Literacy in India, http://www.census2011.co.in/literacy.php.

India, G.o. (2011e). Stamp Duties, in: Department of Revenue, M.o.F. (Ed.), http://www.dor.gov.in/stamduty.

India,   G.o.   (2013).   Annual   Report   2013-14.   Central   Water   Commision, http://www.cwc.gov.in/main/downloads/Annual%20Report%200402%202013-14.pdf.

India, G.o. (2014a). Annual Report 2013-14, in: Implementation, M.o.S.a.P. (Ed.). Sardar Patel   Bhawan,   Sansad   Marg,   New   Delhi, http://mospi.nic.in/Mospi_New/upload/mospi_annual_report_2013-14.pdf.

India, G.o. (2014b). The Right to Fair Compensation and Transparency in Land Acquisition, Rehabilitation and Resettlement Act, 2013, in: Ministry of Rural Development, D.o.L.R.   (Ed.), http://dolr.nic.in/dolr/downloads/pdfs/Right%20to%20Fair%20Compensation%20an d%20Transparency%20in%20Land%20Acquisition,%20Rehabilitation%20and%20R esettlement%20Act,%202013.pdf.

India,   G.o.   (2015a).   National   Commission   of   Scheduled   Tribes, http://www.ncst.nic.in/index.asp?langid=1.

India, G.o. (2015b). The Right to Fair Compensation and Transparency in Land Acquisition, Rehabilitation and Resettlement (RFCTLARR) (Amendment) Ordinance, 2015, in: Ministry   of   Rural   Development,   D.o.L.R.   (Ed.), http://dolr.nic.in/dolr/downloads/pdfs/RFCTLARR%20Act%20%28Amendment%29 %20Second%20Ordinance,%202015.pdf.

Iyer, R.R. (2007). Towards a Just Displacement and Rehabilitation Policy. *Economic and Political Weekly* 42, 3103-7.

J.O'S. (2015). The Fight over India's Land Laws, *The Economist Explains*. The Economist, Online.

Jaamdar, S.M. (2006). The Upper Krishna Project: Recent Improvements, but Resettlements still Elusive, in: Mathur, H.M. (Ed.), *Managing Resettlement in India: Approaches, Issues, Experiences.* Oxford University Press, New Delhi, India, pp. 304-15.

Jacobs, H.M. (2006). The" Taking" of Europe, Globalizing the American Ideal of Private Property? Lincoln Institute of Land Policy, Cambridge, USA, p. 97.

Joskow, P.L. (1988). Asset Specificity and the Structure of Vertical Relationships: Empirical Evidence. *Journal of Law, Economics, & Organization* 4, 95-117.

Kanbur, R. (2003). Development Economics and the Compensation Principle. *International Social Science Journal* 55, 27-35.

Karnataka, G.o. Raitamitra: Rainfall, in: Agriculture, K.S.D.o. (Ed.), http://raitamitra.kar.nic.in/agriprofile/rainfall.htm.

Karnataka, G.o. (2004). 40 Years of Upper Krishna Project, in: Limited, K.B.J.N. (Ed.). Government of Karnataka, Bangalore, India, pp. 1-321.

Karnataka, G.o. (2005). Brief Status Report of Upper Krishna Project for the Year 2005-06, in: Office, L.A. (Ed.), Bagalkot, Karnataka.

Karnataka, G.o. (2006). Karnataka - Upper Krishna Project III: Economic Rehabilitation of Project Affected Population (Action Plan I), in: Revenue Department, U. (Ed.). Government of Karnataka, Navanagar, Bagalkot, pp. 1-77.

Karnataka, G.o. (2008). UKP Implementation Report, Bangalore, India.

Karnataka, G.o. (2011). Annual Plan 2011-12, http://planningcommission.nic.in/plans/stateplan/present/Karnataka.pdf.

Karnataka, G.o. (2012). Land Acquisition, and Rehabilitation and Resettlement Component of UKP stages - I, II, and III, in: Ltd., K.B.J.N. (Ed.), Bangalore.

Karnataka, G.o. (2013a). Base-line Socio Economic Survey for Implementation of UKP stage-III: A Status Report, in: Research, C.f.M.a.S. (Ed.). KBJNL Bangalore.

Karnataka, G.o. (2013b). Upper Krishna Project Brief Report until end of September 2013, in: Bagalkot, O.o.C.R.R.a.L. (Ed.), Bagalkot, pp. 1-7.

Karnataka, G.o. (2014). Annual Report 2013-14. Krishna Bagya Jala Nigam Ltd. , http://www.kbjnl.com/sites/default/files/KBJNL_ANNUAL_20TH_REPORT_Eng.pdf.

Karnataka, G.o. (2015a). Acts and Rules: Stamp Duty, in: Registration, D.o.S.a. (Ed.), https://www.karnataka.gov.in/karigr/actsrules/stampduty/default.htm.

Karnataka, G.o. (2015b). Economic Survey Reports 2014-2015 English, http://planning.kar.nic.in/survey_2015_eng.html.

Kockelman, K.M., Podgorski, K., Bina, M., Gadda, S. (2012). Public Perceptions of Pricing Existing Roads and other Transportation Policies: The Texas Perspective, *Journal of the Transportation Research Forum.*

Lejano, R.P., Shankar, S. (2013). The Contextualist Turn and Schematics of Institutional Fit: Theory and a Case Study from Southern India. *Policy Sciences* 46, 83-102.

Libecap, G.D. (1986). Property Rights in Economic History: Implications for Research. *Explorations in Economic History* 23, 227-52.

Libecap, G.D. (1989). Distributional Issues in Contracting for Property Rights. *Journal of Institutional and Theoretical Economics (JITE)/Zeitschrift für die gesamte Staatswissenschaft*, 6-24.

Libecap, G.D. (1993). *Contracting for Property Rigths.* Cambridge University Press.

Long, J.S., Freese, J. (2014). *Regression Models for Categorical Dependent Variables Using Stata*, Third ed. Stata Press, Texas, USA.

Lueck, D., Miceli, T.J. (2004). Property Rights and Property Law, *Handbook of Law and Economics* Polinsky & Shavell, eds.,.

Lueck, D., Miceli, T.J. (2007). Property Law, in: Polinsky, A.M., Shavell, S. (Eds.), *Handbook of Law and Economics*. Elsevier, pp. 183-257.

Mahapatra, A., Mitchell, C. (2001). Classifying Tree Planters and Non Planters in a Subsistence Farming System Using a Discriminant Analytical Approach. *Agroforestry Systems* 52, 41-52.

Mann, C., Absher, J.D. (2014). Adjusting Policy to Institutional, Cultural and Biophysical Context Conditions: The Case of Conservation Banking in California. *Land Use Policy* 36, 73-82.

MapsofIndia.com (2012). Indian Map.

Marjit, S. (2010). Guaranteeing Future Claims of Farmers in Land Acquisition: An Option-pricing Approach. *Economic and Political Weekly* 45, 80-2.

Mathur, H.M. (2006a). Introduction and Overview, in: Mathur, H.M. (Ed.), *Managing Resttlement in India: Approaches, Issues, Experiences*. Oxford University Press, New Delhi, India, pp. 1-18.

Mathur, H.M. (2006b). New Livelihoods for Old: Restoring Incomes Lost due to Involuntary Resettlement, in: Mathur, H.M. (Ed.), *Managing Resttlement in India: Approaches, Issues, Experiences*. Oxford University Press, New Delhi, India, pp. 67-98.

Mathur, H.M. (2006c). Resettling People Displaced by Development Projects: Some Critical Management Issues. *Social Change* 36, 36-86.

McElwee, G., Smith, R. (2012). Classifying the Strategic Capability of Farmers: A Segmentation Framework. *International Journal of Entrepreneurial Venturing* 4, 111-31.

McGinnis, M.D. (2011). An Introduction to IAD and the Language of the Ostrom Workshop: A Simple Guide to a Complex Framework. *Policy Studies Journal* 39, 169-83.

Mearns, R., Binns, T. (1995). Institutions and Natural Resource Management: Access to and Control over Woodfuel in East Africa. *People and Environment in Africa.*, 103-14.

Meinzen-Dick, R. (2014). Property Rights and Sustainable Irrigation: A Developing Country Perspective. *Agricultural Water Management*.

Ménard, C. (2004). The Economics of Hybrid Organizations. *Journal of Institutional and Theoretical Economics* 160, 345-76.

Merriam-Webster (2004). *Merriam-Webster's Collegiate Dictionary*. Merriam-Webster Inc.

Miceli, T.J., Segerson, K. (2000). Takings. *Encyclopedia of Law and Economics* 4, 328-57.

Misri, B.K. (2006). Country Pasture / Forage Resources Profiles - India. Food and Agriculture Organization (FAO), http://www.fao.org/ag/agp/AGPC/doc/Counprof/India/India.htm.

Moss, T. (2012). Spatial Fit, from Panacea to Practice: Implementing the EU Water Framework Directive. *Ecology and Society* 17, 2.

Musole, M. (2009). Property Rights, Transaction Costs and Institutional Change: Conceptual Framework and Literature Review. *Progress in Planning* 71, 43-85.

Nagaraja, B., Somashekar, R., Kavitha, A. (2010). Impact of Drought on Agriculture: Challenges Facing Poor Farmers of Karnataka, South India. *climsec.prio.no/papers/climatechangenorwayfinalpaper.pdf*.

Nayak, A.K. (2010). Big Dams and Protests in India: A Study of Hirakud Dam. *Economic and Political Weekly* 45, 69-73.

Nielsen, H.Ø., Frederiksen, P., Saarikoski, H., Rytkönen, A.-M., Pedersen, A.B. (2013). How Different Institutional Arrangements Promote Integrated River Basin Management. Evidence from the Baltic Sea Region. *Land Use Policy* 30, 437-45.

North, D.C. (1994). Institutional Change: A Framework of Analysis. *Economic History* 9412001.

Öhlmér, B., Olson, K., Brehmer, B. (1998). Understanding Farmers' Decision Making Processes and Improving Managerial Assistance. *Agricultural Economics* 18, 273-90.

Organization, W.H. WHO: The Lexicon.

Ostrom, E. (1990). *Governing the Commons: The Evolution of Institutions for Collective Action.* Cambridge University Press.

Ostrom, E. (2007). A Diagnostic Approach for Going Beyond Panaceas. *Proceedings of the National Academy of Sciences* 104, 15181-7.

Ostrom, E. (2008). The Challenge of Common-pool Resources. *Environment: Science and Policy for Sustainable Development* 50, 8-21.

Ostrom, E. (2011). Background on the Institutional Analysis and Development Framework. *Policy Studies Journal* 39, 7-27.

Ostrom, E., Hess, C. (2008). Private and Common Property Rights, in: Bouckaert, B. (Ed.), *Property Law and Economics*, 2 ed. Edward Elgar Publishing, Inc., Massachusetts, USA, p. 53.

Ostrom, E., Janssen, M.A., Anderies, J.M. (2007). Going Beyond Panaceas. *Proceedings of the National Academy of Sciences* 104, 15176-8.

Pammachius (2011). Involuntary Transactions Destroy Wealth, *Liberty and Prosperity: The More of One, the More of the Other*, Online.

Pandey, A., Morris, S. (2007). Towards Reform of Land Acquisition Framework in India. *Economic and Political Weekly* 42, 2083-90.

Parasuraman, S. (1996). Development Projects, Displacement and Outcomes for Displaced: Two Case Studies. *Economic and Political Weekly* 31, 1529-32.

Pradhan, R., Pradhan, U. (2000). Negotiating Access and Rights: Disputes Over Rights to an Irrigation Water Source in Nepal, in: Bruns, B.R., Meinzen-Dick, R.S. (Eds.), *Negotiating Water Rights*. Intermediate Technology Press, London, pp. 200-21.

Prager, K. (2010). Applying the Institutions of Sustainability Framework to the Case of Agricultural Soil Conservation. *Environmental Policy and Governance* 20, 223-38.

Prager, K., Hagemann, N., Schuler, J., Heyn, N. (2011a). Incentives and Enforcement: The Institutional Design and Policy Mix for Soil Conservation in Brandenburg (Germany). *Land Degradation and Development* 22, 111-23.

Prager, K., Schuler, J., Helming, K., Zander, P., Ratinger, T., Hagedorn, K. (2011b). Soil degradation, farming practices, institutions and policy responses: An analytical framework. *Land Degradation & Development* 22, 32-46.

Profit, N. (2013a). Land Acquisition Bill to Hit Project Timelines, Hike Cost Estimates: Crisil, *Press Trust of India*, New Delhi.

Profit, N. (2013b). Land Acquisition Cost may Go up to 3.5 Times: India Inc, *Press Trust of India*. Press Trust of India, New Delhi.

Profit, N. (2013c). Land Bill: Prices to Rise, Acquisition to Take Time, says FICCI, *Press Trust of India*. Press Trust of India, New Delhi.

Ramachandra, T.V., Kamakshi, G., Shruthi, B.V. (2004). Bioresource status in Karnataka. *Renewable and Sustainable Energy Reviews* 8, 1-47.

Ramaswamy, R.I. (2009). A Slow but Sure Step Forward *The Hindu*, Online edition of India's National Newspaper ed. The Hindu Group, India.

Ranganathan, V. (2010). Challenges of Land Acquisition. *Economic and Political Weekly* 45, 39-41.

Ray, S.C. (2010). From Detroit to Singur: On the Question of Land Acquisition for Private Development, May 2010 ed. University of Connecticut.

Reddy, V.R., Reddy, B.S. (2007). Land Alienation and Local Communities: Case Studies in Hyderabad-Secunderabad. *Economic and Political Weekly* 42, 3233-40.

Ribot, J.C. (1998). Theorizing Access: Forest Profits along Senegal's Charcoal Commodity Chain. *Development and Change* 29, 307-41.

Ribot, J.C., Peluso, N.L. (2003). A Theory of Access*. *Rural sociology* 68, 153-81.

Rindfleisch, A., Heide, J.B. (1997). Transaction Cost Analysis: Past, Present, and Future Applications. *The Journal of Marketing*, 30-54.

Robinson, W.C. (2003). *Risks and Rights: The Causes, Consequences, and Challenges of Development-induced Displacement.* Brookings Institution Washington, DC.

Salem, B. (1989). *Arid Zone Forestry: A Guide for Field Technicians.* Food and Agriculture Organization (FAO).

Sampat, P. (2013). Limits to Absolute Power–Eminent Domain and the Right to Land in India. *Economic and Political Weekly* 48, 40-52.

Saxena, N.C. (2006). The Resettlement and Rehabilitation Policy of India, in: Mathur, H.M. (Ed.), *Managing Resettlement in India: Approaches, Issues and Experiences.* Oxford University Press, New Delhi, pp. 99-123.

Schlager, E., Ostrom, E. (1992). Property-Rights Regimes and Natural Resources: A Conceptual Analysis. *Land Economics* 68, 249-62.

Sen, A. (2008). Capability and Well-being, in: Hausman, D.M. (Ed.), *The Philosophy of Economics: An Anthology.* Cambridge University Press, United States of America, New York, pp. 270-93.

Serageldin, I. (2006). Involuntary Resettlement in World Bank-Financed Projects: Reducing Impoverishment Risks for the Affected People, in: Mathur, H.M. (Ed.), *Managing Resttlement in India: Approaches, Issues, Experiences.* Oxford University Press, New Delhi, India, pp. 45-66.

Shah, A. (2010). Development-induced Displacement in Gujarat. *Economic and Political Weekly* 45, 37-8.

Sheikh, A.D., Rehman, T., Yates, C.M. (2003). Logit Models for Identifying the Factors that Influence the Uptake of New 'No-tillage' Technologies by Farmers in the Rice - Wheat and the Cotton - Wheat Farming Systems of Pakistan's Punjab. *Agricultural Systems* 75, 79-95.

Shiddalingaswami, H., Raghavendra, V.K. (2010). Regional Disparities in Karnataka: a District Level Analysis of Growth and Development, *Monograph - 60.* Centre For Multi-Disciplinary Development Research (CMDR), Dharwad.

Shirley, M.M., Ménard, C. (2005). *Handbook of New Institutional Economics.* Springer.

Singh, R. (2012). Inefficiency and Abuse of Compulsory Land Acquisition. *Economic and Political Weekly* 47, 46-53.

Society, A.M. (2012). Glossary of Meteorology.

Stanley, J. (2000). Development-induced Displacement and Resettlement. forcedmigration.org.

Stanley, J. (2004). Development-induced Displacement and Resettlement *Expert Guides.*

Sud, N. (2014). Governing India's Land. *World Development* 60, 43-56.

Terminski, B. (2013). *Development-Induced Displacement and Resettlement: Theoretical Frameworks and Current Challenges.* University of Geneva, Geneva, Switzerland.

Tribunal, K.W.D. (2010). The Report of the Krishna Water Disputes Tribunal with the Decision in: India, S.C.o. (Ed.), New Delhi, pp. 1-213.

Tripathi, A., Prasad, A. (2009). Agricultural Development in India since Independence: A Study on Progress, Performance, and Determinants. *Journal of Emerging Knowledge on Emerging Markets* 1.

UNEP, Council, W.S.S.C., Organization, W.H. (1997). *Water Pollution Control - A Guide to the Use of Water Quality Management Principles* 2ed. E & FN Spon, London.

Vanslembrouck, I., Van Huylenbroeck, G., Verbeke, W. (2002). Determinants of the Willingness of Belgian Farmers to Participate in Agri-environmental Measures. *Journal of Agricultural Economics* 53, 489-511.

Vatn, A., Vedeld, P. (2012). Fit, Interplay, and Scale: A Diagnosis. *Ecology and Society* 17, 12.

Veettil, P.C., Kjosavik, D.J., Ashok, A. (2013). Valuing the 'Bundle of Land Rights': On Formalising Indigenous People's (Adivasis) Land Rights in Kerala, India. *Land Use Policy* 30, 408-16.

Verspecht, A., Vandermeulen, V., De Bolle, S., Moeskops, B., Vermang, J., Van den Bossche, A., Van Huylenbroeck, G., De Neve, S. (2011). Integrated Policy Approach to Mitigate Soil Erosion in West Flanders. *Land Degradation and Development* 22, 84-96.

Vyas, A., Mahalingam, A. (2011). Comparative Evaluation of Land Acquisition and Compensation Processes across the World. *Economic and Political Weekly* 46, 94-102.

Williamson, O.E. (1979). Transaction Cost Economics: The Governance of Contractual Relations. *Journal of Law and Economics* 22, 233-61.

Williamson, O.E. (1981). The Economics of Organization: The Transaction Cost Approach. *American Journal of Sociology*, 548-77.

Williamson, O.E. (1985). *The Economic Institutions of Capitalism: Firms, markets, relational Contracting*. The Free Press, New York.

Williamson, O.E. (1987a). *Antitrust Economics: Mergers, Contracting, and Strategic Behavior*. Basil Blackwell Oxford.

Williamson, O.E. (1987b). Transaction Cost Economics: The Comparative Contracting Perspective. *Journal of Economic Behavior and Organization* 8, 617-25.

Williamson, O.E. (1991). Comparative Economic Organization: The analysis of Discrete Structural Alternatives. *Administrative Science Quarterly* 36, 269-96.

Williamson, O.E. (1996). *The Mechanisms of Governance*. Oxford University Press.

Williamson, O.E. (1998). Transaction Cost Economics: How It Works; Where It is Headed. *De Economist* 146, 23-58.

Williamson, O.E. (2003). Transaction Cost Economics and Economic Sociology, *CSES Working Paper Series*. Cornell University, Ithaca, NY 14853-7601.

Williamson, O.E. (2005). The Economics of Governance. *American Economic Review*, 1-18.

World Bank, R. (1998). Recent Experience with Involuntary Resettlement India - Upper Krishna (Karnataka and Maharashtra). World Bank pp. 1-44.

Young, O.R. (2002). *The Institutional Dimensions of Environmental Change: Fit, Interplay, and Scale*. MIT press, Cambridge, Massachusetts, USA.

Young, O.R. (2008). The Architecture of Global Environmental Governance: Bringing Science to Bear on Policy. *Global Environmental Politics* 8, 14-32.

Zbinden, S., Lee, D.R. (2005). Paying for Environmental Services: An Analysis of Participation in Costa Rica's PSA Program. *World Development* 33, 255-72.

Zikos, D., Roggero, M. (2013). The Patronage of Thirst: Exploring Institutional Fit on a Fivided Cyprus. *Ecology and Society* 18, 25.

Annexure

A. Description about Interviews with the Government Officials

Table A1: Sample list of interviews with the government officials

S.N.	Respondent Name	Designation	Date	Interviewer
1	S.M. Jaamdar	Ex-special commissioner, UKP, R&R	23.06.2012	Vikram Patil
2	Doddabasavaraj	Ex-special Rehabilitation Officer	10.05.2012	Vikram Patil
3	Kunjappa	District Commissioner and in-charge General Manager, R&R office, Bagalkot	05.03.2012	Vikram Patil
4	Madan Naik	Deputy General Manager, R&R office, Bagalkot	15.04.2012	Vikram Patil
5	Sanmuk	Special Land Acquisition Officer, SLO office, Bagalkot	08.03.2012	Vikram Patil
6	Sampgavi	R&R Office, Bagalkot	15.03.2012	Vikram Patil
7	Mahesh	R&R office, Bagalkot	15.03.2012	Vikram Patil
8	S.G. Meti	Programmer, R&R Office	18.03.2012	Vikram Patil
9	Hanamanth Reddy	Chief Baseline Surveyor, R&R office	13.05.2012	Vikram Patil
10	M. Joshi	Gazetted Officer, R&R office	01.04.2012	Vikram Patil
11	Shettar	Assistant Engineer, R&R Office	01.03.2012	Vikram Patil
12	Bajanthri	SLO Office	01.04.2012	Vikram Patil
13	Sanjay	SLO Office	05.04.2012	Vikram Patil

I interviewed 13 key government officials. Among them, nine from Rehabilitation Office (RO), Bagalkot and three from Special Land Acquisition Office (SLO), Bagalkot and one special rehabilitation officer. Among these, I interviewed a retired special commissioner of the UKP, Mr. Jamadar who was assigned special powers to make changes in policy and administration. He made major policy changes in favor of project displaced families. The name and details of the interviewees are listed in Table A1.

In the interviews, I discussed about land acquisition and displacement procedures and their changes over the period or stages of the project, consent award and general award, farmers' resistance towards the displacement, experiences in implementing and organizing the rehabilitation process, apportionment of compensation and its issues, name of the villages where displacement has badly affected the farmers' livelihood, etc.

A brief highlights of some of the responses and observations of interviews:

1. Regarding the policy changes: In early stage of displacement, the government had made compensation apportionment only through general award. During that period, rent seeking of the middlemen like lawyers increased. Farmers were exploited by these people. In order to avoid this rent seeking behavior as well as for those who are unable to approach court in case of the general award, government at local level brought consent award. In consent award, for immovable structures, compensation was provided as per the valuation of amount based on Daily Schedule of Rates (DSR) plus 50 per cent of that total amount. Based on local market value of the land, certain amount is fixed by discussing with displaced people for lands. Consent was taken from the farmers to not to approach the court for claiming further compensation. During this stage, Major farmers opted for the consent award. This concept of consent award in the UKP was a major breakthrough in fastening the project implementation.

2. Consent award started with fixing the land rates village wise based on local market value and type of land. Later there was lot of resistance by the farmers, farmers started behaving opportunistically, and government officials also started seeking rent from the farmers for increasing the consent award. Then government made a declaration of single consent award for entire project irrespective of villages and location. But, consent award was fixed separately for dry land, irrigated land, single cropped and double cropped lands.

3. However, in later stages, rent seeking lawyers started forcing/convincing the farmers to opt for the general award. This they did by attracting the farmers by giving slightly more amount than the consent award and making them to select general award. The lawyers claimed themselves higher compensation either by running the cases in the civil court or by approaching high court. For example, suppose the consent award is 200,000 rupees per acre of land and initial base amount in the general award 100,000 rupees per acre. The lawyer will approach the farmer and make an agreement with him to opt the general award by paying him 250000 rupees per acre. Then lawyer take the benefit of whatever the higher compensation he gets through litigation in later stages.

4. Regarding land transactions: during the early stage, slope of the demand curve of land in surrounding area of the UKP was less and the sellers were very little aware of these price announcements and other information regarding the displacement. Even after the announcement of the award, there were very little changes in the land prices. Thus, farmers those who want to continue in agriculture were able to repurchase at least some portion of land after their displacement with their compensation amount. But, after the year 2000, the slope of the demand curve of land started becoming steeper. In addition, seller farmers were more informed about price announcements in the project. As soon as the award was announced, the sellers increased the land prices higher than the consent award. Thus, majority of the small farmers did not able to repurchase the land and majority among those who have repurchased the land were able to purchase only less than the earlier holding.

5. Government officials' response for land for land provision: This provision is possible only by acquiring farmers' land in the surrounding non-submergence area. By doing this, the number of farmers affect from the UKP will be doubled and work for the project will also be doubled. Project will be further delayed and incur high transaction cost.

6. Even if the farmers did not get the land after displacement, they are practicing *dradoon cultivation* in their original land and taking single crop. Water stagnates in the submerged lands only for three to four months in a year. After it drains out of the field, farmers will come and cultivate a crop. However, this type of cultivation is temporary and soon after completion of the final stage of the project, this is also not possible for those farmers. Because the land will be submerged for longer period in a year. These farmers have not realized this situation yet. They will be affected badly.

7. Government has created some of the rehabilitation centers near to the cities with an intention that displaced people will get an employment. They hardly got any employment other than construction and road labor work because of the lack of the skills. Despite the government has given the some employment training programs, it has given very less importance to employment generation. As a result, the farmers' livelihood became unstable.

8. I visited two villages. I found that infrastructure wise the displaced villages are better off as compared to earlier displaced villages and nearby villages. Land availability and lack of portfolio management are the main problems for these farmers. Therefore, lot of miss-utilization of compensation amount has taken place by the displaced farmers with some exceptional cases. Somehow, they are cultivating the earlier land and they

are taking single crop now. However, their situation will be hard in near future after the completion of final stage.

9. One more interesting thing is some farmers / villages, who were not under the submergence jurisdictions, went to the government to consider them under submergence. Instead of resistance, some farmers went government officials in want of compensation. This was mainly because of the perception that they can get higher compensation as well as can continue cultivating the same land.

10. Till date, there was no strong resistance / protest against the project or against the loop holes of the rehabilitation policy as such. According to some officials, I found out indirectly that this might be because of lack of capable leaders to raise an issue and lack awareness among the displaced people.

Interview questions with Ex-Special commissioner, R&R, UKP

1. When did the UKP start implementing?

2. Sir I have confused with the stages and phases of the project. Please would you explain them in detail about these stages and phases?

3. What each stage/phase consists of? (What has been done in each stage/phase?)

4. What is the Benefit-Lost ratio? (i.e., how much irrigated land and how much dry land submerged and how much land has been irrigated, how much population affected and how much population got benefited?)

5. How R&R policy of the UKP changed over the period of time/ over the subsequent stages/phases related to agricultural land?

6. What are the difficulties/issues you have faced in implementing the R&R policy related to land?

7. How did you tackle these issues?

8. What is consent award? On what bases the amount in this award was fixed?

9. When and why did the Consent Award come into existence?

10. What was the farmers' response to the CA?

11. What is the impact of the CA on both the project and the PDFs?

12. What was the purpose of the compensation amount for land in general and consent in particular? Was it to help the PDFs in repurchasing land?

13. What are the drawbacks of the General Award?

14. What are the drawbacks of the Consent award?

15. As soon as the compensation award is announced (4(1) notification) and project started implementing, the land prices shoot up. By the time farmers get the compensation amount, the price per unit of land will be more than compensation given. Therefore, they end up either with less land or with no land. Whatever high compensation amount you give this cycle of price boom will continue. What are your opinion / insights to this issue?

16. What are the other flaws in the policy, which policy makers should deal with?

17. What was the farmers' response in the initial stage of the project and how did it change over the period?

HUMBOLDT-UNIVERSITÄT ZU BERLIN

FACULTY OF AGRICULTURE AND HORTICULTURE

Department of Agricultural Economics | Division of Resource Economics | Prof. Dr. Dr. h.c. Konrad Hagedorn

17.01.2016

B. Questionnaire for Interviews with Government officials

Project Title: Governing Involuntary Land Transactions: Insights from Irrigation Projects in
India
Information sought for PhD research in Agricultural Economics by
Mr. Vikram Patil (MSc. Ag) PhD Scholar
Dept. of Agricultural Economics, Humboldt University, Berlin.
Email ID: vickyagrico@gmail.com

1. What is the procedure for Displacement / Rehabilitation of farmers?

_____
_____
_____
_____

2. Are there any changes in the current displacement process as compared to previous process?
   Yes ▣   No ▣
3. If Yes, What changes?

_____
_____
_____
_____

4. a. What is your experience in implementing and organizing the Rehabilitation of farmers?
   b. What is the impact now?

_____
_____
_____
_____
_____

5. Can I get list of villages displaced?
   If yes, to whom to contact? _____

6. Give some village names, which are successful in displacement and/or rehabilitation?

_____
_____

_____

_____

_____

7. Give some villages names, which are not successful in displacement and/or rehabilitation?

_____

_____

_____

_____

8. What are the reasons for successful and unsuccessful rehabilitation?

_____

_____

_____

_____

9. Can I get village wise list of farmers with their land holding, actual land submerged, and other details? (Area in Ha/acre)
   If yes, to whom to contact? _____

10. What is the per cent of farmers who opt for General award? (Who went to court to claim their compensation)

_____

_____

_____

11. What was the compensation amount given for different types of land? On which basis?

_____

_____

_____

12. What is General Award and Consent Award?

_____

_____

_____

13. Can I get village wise list of farmers who opt for General Award?
    If yes, to whom to contact? _____

_____

14.   Were there any protests happened by the farmers during the displacement?
Yes   ▓   No   ▓

15.   If Yes, for which reasons?

_____

_____

_____

Thank you very much for giving your valuable time in your busy schedule and sharing your experience and information with me.

C. Questions: Focus Group Interviews

1. Share your experiences in shifting to and settling in new place.

2. How you have shifted to new place?

3. What were the problems faced during the displacement?

4. What were the problems in purchasing the land?

5. What you think about why land prices increased?

6. Why land purchasing is so difficult in the area?

7. Did the government offer you to provide the land?

8. Why you were not able purchase the land?

9. If you have purchased the land, what are all you need to do from point of searching the land until purchase?

10. How much time it took you to purchase the land?

11. How you are feeling about the new place, livelihood, and land assets compared to your earlier village?

HUMBOLDT-UNIVERSITÄT ZU BERLIN

FACULTY OF AGRICULTURE AND HORTICULTURE

Department of Agricultural Economics | Division of Resource Economics | Prof. Dr. Dr. h.c. Konrad Hagedorn

17.01.2016

Requisition Letter

From,

    Mr. Vikram Patil (MSc. Ag)
    PhD Scholar
    Dept. of Agricultural Economics,
    Division of Resource Economics,
    Humboldt University, Berlin.

To,

  GMO
  UKP R&R Office,
  Bagalkot.

Subject: Seeking documents regarding R&R, UKP for PhD research.

Respected Sir,

I, Vikram Patil doing doctoral studies in Humboldt University, Berlin. For my PhD dissertation, I have chosen a research on Institutions, Institutional Changes in the Rehabilitation of Displaced Farmers: The Case of the Upper Krishna Irrigation Project, India. Hence, I am seeking documents regarding formal organizational and other related aspects of Rehabilitation and Resettlement program of the Upper Krishna Irrigation Project. The aim of the study is to analyze the organizational processes and issues or R&R program and their impacts on the displaced farmers. Here with I request you to kindly provide below mentioned and their related documents. This will be great help for me. Along with this letter, I also provide letter of commitment saying that the given data will not be misused.

Thanking you in advance.

Documents: 1. R&R formal procedure from land acquisition until displacement and rehabilitation.

    2. Village wise list of farmers with actual landholding, land submerged, award taken (Consent/General) and other related information.

    3. Other R&R related information, pictures, and videos if any.

Your Sincerely,
Vikram Patil

FACULTY OF AGRICULTURE AND HORTICULTURE

Department of Agricultural Economics | Division of Resource Economics | Prof. Dr. Dr. h.c. Konrad Hagedorn

17.01.2016

Letter of Commitment

To whoever it is concerned

The information sought regarding formal organizational and other related aspects of Rehabilitation and Resettlement Program of the Upper Krishna Irrigation Project will be used for my PhD research on Institutions, Institutional Changes in the Rehabilitation of Displaced Farmers: The Case of the Upper Krishna Irrigation Project, India. The aim of the study is to analyze the organizational processes and issues of R&R program and their impacts on the displaced farmers. Here with I commit that the interview data will be anonymized and special caution will be exercised in order to prevent negative consequences for anybody involved. The name and other personal information of the interviewees will not be published anywhere.

Thank you for giving your valuable time and providing information.

With kind regards,
Mr. Vikram Patil (MSc. Ag)
PhD Scholar
Dept. of Agricultural Economics,
Division of Resource Economics,
Humboldt University, Berlin.

HUMBOLDT-UNIVERSITÄT ZU BERLIN

FACULTY OF AGRICULTURE AND HORTICULTURE

Department of Agricultural Economics | Division of Resource Economics | Prof. Dr. Dr.
h.c. Konrad Hagedorn

17.01.2016

D. Questionnaire: Farmers' Interviews

Survey on Farmers' Decision towards Compensation Claim Mechanisms

Principal Investigator

Mr. Vikram Patil (MSc. Ag)

PhD Scholar

Dept. of Agricultural Economics,

Humboldt University, Berlin.

Email: vikram.patil.1@agrar.hu-berlin.de; vspatil.6@gmail.com

Panel Identification

Code: _____ Investigator: _____ Supervisor: _____

Date: _____ Starting Time: _____ Ending Time: _____

Village: _____ Mandal: _____ District: _____
       (Taluk)

1. **General details**

    Name of the respondent   :

    Age   :

    Education   : _____ (No. of years of schooling)

                Specialization (if any) _____

    Occupation   :

    Caste   :

    Year of compensation   :

    Year of displacement   :

    Contact number   :

2. **a) Type of family: i) Before Displacement: Nuclear ☐   Joint ☐**

        ii) After Displacement: Nuclear ☐   Joint ☐

    b) How many people were staying in house before displacement?
_____

    c) Current family details

Sl. No	Name	Relation with head	Age	Sex	Educational status	Main occupation	Sub occupation (in case of non-farm income)
1.							
2.							
3.							
4.							
5.							
6.							

Relation with head: D = Daughter; S = Son; M = Mother; F = Father; Sis = Sister and Br = Brother and Oth = Others.

3. Did you know that there were two options (Consent Award (CA) and General Award (GA)) for claiming compensation? (Local Names: Oppige Eithirpu for CA and Samanya Eithirpu for GA).

Yes ☐   No ☐

If answer to question no. 3 above is yes, then answer questions 5, 6, 8 and 9:
4. How did you claim the compensation?
Consent Award ☐   General Award ☐   Both ☐

5. Reasons for your choice

　　¤

_____
_____
_____

6. Who convinced/ forced you to choose the particular award? And why?

　　¤

Own decision ☐   Lawyers ☐   Friends ☐   Relatives ☐

_____
_____
_____

7. Did you take anybody's help in claiming the compensation amount?

　　¤

Yes ☐   No ☐

8. If yes, whose (Like local leader, politician or others)?

　　_____

9. Were you a member of panchayat/society/cooperatives/boards/others?

Yes ☐   No ☐

10. If yes, institutional participation/member of

Gram Panchayat ☐   Taluk Panchayat ☐   Zilla Panchayat ☐

Dairy co-operative ☐   Co-op society   ☐   Any Political party ☐

11. What compensation you received per acre of land? In how many instalments?

Rs._____   No. _____

12. Did you have to spend some money in the claiming process?

Yes ☐   No ☐

13. If yes, for what purpose and how much?

_____

Rs. _____

14. How much time you have spent in getting compensation – on different occasions?

_____ Hours / Days / Months / Years

15. Before you chose the award, did you know how much minimum time it could have taken to seek the compensation in case of general award?

Yes ☐   No ☐

16. Did you face any problems while getting compensation?

_____
_____
_____

17. Did you face any problems after displacement?

_____
_____

18. Did you want to continue in agriculture / farming after displacement?

Yes ☐   No ☐

19. What is your main source of income now?

Agriculture ☐   Others (mention) ☐

20. Land Holding Particulars (in Acres/Guntas)

Sl. No	Type of Land	Owned	Submerged area	No. of fragments	Leased in	Leased out	Market value (Rs/acre)	Rent per acre
A.	Before displacement							
1.	Dry land							
2.	Canal/ River Irrigated							
3.	Irrigated by well							
4.	Total							
B.	After displacement (current holding)							
1.	Dry land							
2.	Canal/ River Irrigated							
3.	Irrigated by well							
4.	Total							

21. Location and Type of Land

Particulars	Survey No. of Field	Distance from canal /river (feet / Km)	Road connectivity	Distance from the main road (Km)	Soil type	Soil fertility
Old Land						
New Land						

Old Land: submerged land; New land: newly purchased land after displacement.

22. How did you spend your compensation amount?

Land ☐   Others ☐   Both ☐

23. If you have not purchased land, what are the reasons for doing so?

_____

_____

_____

_____

24. If you have purchased land less than your submerged land, what are the reasons?

_____

_____

25. Dispersion of Compensation Amount on Different Activities

Sl. No.	Activities	Quantity	Investment made in Rs.	Year
a.	**Income Generating Activities**			
1.	Agricultural Land			
2.	Livestock			
3.	Shops			
4.	Bank Deposits			
5.	Sites			
6.	Capital Equipments			
7.	Other Financial Instruments*			
8.	Other Business			
b.	**Non-income Generating Activities**			
a)	Ceremonies			
b)	Vehicles			
c)	Previous Loan			
d)	House construction			
e)	Others			

*Financial instruments = Shares, Bonds, Monetary gold, securities, etc.

26. If you have purchased land, when did you get it after you received the compensation?

_____ months / years.

27. If you have purchased the land, price per acre: Rs._____

28. Type of Land:

Dry Land ☐   River/Canal Irrigated ☐   Borewell Irrigated ☐   Others ☐

29. What is its distance from your new home?

_____ Meters/Km.

30. How is the purchased land as compared to submerged land in terms of fertility, location, soil type, and shape?

Better ☐   Same ☐   Almost same ☐   Not better ☐   Worst ☐

31. Why do you think so? Give 2-3 reasons at least?

_____
_____
_____
_____

32. What has been the loss / gain for having lost your land – your estimation of this loss / gain with reason/s?

_____
_____
_____

33. What are your plans of coping with the loss / gain including farm management efforts

_____
_____
_____

34. How did you purchase the land?

Through agent ☐   Personal communication with seller ☐   Others (mention) ☐

_____
_____

35. In case through agent, how much amount did you pay for him? Rs._____.

_____.

36. What are the issues you have faced in land purchases? (in terms of land availability, prices, location, and distance from new home, etc.)

_____
_____
_____
_____

37. Farm Inventory

Sl. No.	Farm assets	No.	Year of purchase / construction	Investment (Rs.)	Annual income from hiring-out machinery (Rs.)	Annual maintenance cost (Rs.)
1	Tractor and its accessories					
2	Sprayers					
3	Bullock cart (Wooden/tire)					
4	Irrigation pump set					
5	Irrigation well					

38. Livestock

Sl. No.	Particulars	No.	Year of purchase	Purchase Value (Rs.)	Present Value (Rs.)	Total earnings (Rs. per year)	Annual maintenance cost (Rs.)
1.	Cows – Crossbred						
2.	Cows – local						
3.	Bullocks Pair						
4.	She Buffaloes						
5.	Sheep						
6.	Goat						
7.	Poultry						
8	Pig / others (specify)						

39. Farm Buildings

Sl. No.	Particulars	Type of building	Year of construction	Cost of construction	Value in 2013

(Type of buildings: Livestock shed, farm/store house or others)

40. Cropping Pattern followed before Displacement

Sl. No	Crop	Area	Yield	Net returns (Rs.)	Irrigation source
A.	Kharif				
1					
2					
3					
B.	Rabi				
1					
2					
3					
C.	Summer				
1					
2					
D.	Perennials				
1					
2					

Irrigation source: Borewell, River, Canal, Tank, open well, others

41. Cropping Pattern followed after Displacement

Sl. No	Crop	Area	Yield	Net returns (Rs.)	Irrigation source
A.	Kharif				
1					
2					
3					
B.	Rabi				
1					
2					
3					
C.	Summer				
1					
2					
D.	Perennials				
1					
2					

Irrigation source: Borewell, River, Canal, Tank, open well, others

42. Sources of Farm- income before and after Displacement

Sl. No.	Enterprise	Before displacement				After displacement			
		No.	GR (Rs)	AMC (Rs)	NR (Rs)	No.	GR (Rs)	AMC (Rs)	NR (Rs)
1	Agriculture								
2	Cow & Buffalo								
4	Poultry								
5	Sheep rearing								
6	Any others (specify)								
	a.								
	b.								

*GR= Gross Returns; AMC = Annual Maintenance cost and NR = Net Returns.

43. Sources of Non-farm Income before and after Displacement

Sl. No.	Source	Before displacement		After displacement	
		Year of start	Annual income (Rs)	Year of start	Annual income(Rs)
1	Salary				
2	Business				
3	Wages				
4	Others (specify)				
	a.				
	b.				

44. Are you still cultivating in your submerged land?

Yes ☐   No ☐

45. If yes, how many crops you are taking there per year?

_____.

46. Farmer's Opinion on Displacement

Indicators	Nature of impact (+ or -)	Scale*	Reasons or remarks for answer
1.Economic impact a) In terms of income			
b) Standard of living			
2. Land availability			
3. Social relationships**			
4. Health hazard***			
5. Social-economic impact in terms of employment generation			

** **Scale:** Not at all =1, Low =2, Moderate= 3, Strong =4; ** Social Relationships = Whether PDF remained as joint family or became nuclear after displacement and whether close relationships with neighboring friends and relatives for day to day activities are maintained after displacement or not. *** Any health imbalances due to/after displacement.*

47. Other General Questions

a. What difference you are seeing in doing agriculture after displacement as compared before?

_____

_____

_____

_____

_____

_____

_____

_____

b. How to improve the Rehabilitation and Resettlement procedure? your suggestions / comments?

_____

_____

_____

c. How to reduce the time component in receiving compensation?

_____

_____

_____

48. Any remarks regarding compensation, displacement, land purchases, etc.?

Thank you very much for spending your valuable time! All the information you have provided will be kept confidential and anonymous and will be used only for research purposes

E. Discrete Choice Modelling Approach

Brief information to the respondents before interview (The enumerators will explain this information verbally before conducting the experiment)
I am a Ph.D. student and am doing research on the Rehabilitation and Resettlement (R&R) issues of Upper Krishna Project. You might be aware that government has notified your land and house and those will be submerged in near future. For that, you will be given compensation and displaced to new place. In that regard, I am trying to find out from the farmers their actual preference for the compensation packages. This is very important information, which is not currently available with anyone. Once we get this, it can be used to help improve the policy.

Therefore, I present you some hypothetical compensation packages for land and house submergence in addition to the status quo government package. I will explain you the status quo compensation package in detail and about the experiment. Please bear with me for some time.

This experiment has nothing to do with the government actions / activities in regard to the displacement and compensation. Your name or information you give will also not be disclosed anywhere and will be used solely for my research purpose. So please feel free to express your preferences. Each option in the choice set includes different provisions. Please carefully observe each option. Imagine that you are in a situation where you are losing completely or part of your property. However, you will be given the following compensation packages by the government.
Please select any one of the package, which you would prefer most. Do let me know if you have any confusion.

There are six types of different compensation packages as follows:

1. **Money + Site (Status quo)** = This has two components: First, cash will be given for lost land on per acre basis. Second, sites and cash for lost house based on the evaluation by the committee will be given.
2. **Money + House** = This has two components: First, Cash will be given for lost land on per acre basis. Second, constructed house in newly allotted village for lost house will be given.

3. **Land + Site** = This has two components: First, land will be given for lost land subjected to ceiling (two acres and remaining cash on per acre basis). Second, sites and cash for lost house based on the evaluation by the committee will be given.

4. **Land + House** = This has two components: First, land will be given for lost land subjected to ceiling (two acres and remaining cash on per acre basis). Second, constructed house in newly allotted village for lost house will be given.

5. **Training for self employment + Site** = This has two components: First, training for self employment with technical and financial assistance for purchase of tools and cash for lost land will be given. Second, sites and cash for lost house based on the evaluation by the committee will be given.

6. **Training for self employment + House** = This has two components: First, training for self employment with technical and financial assistance for purchase of tools and cash for lost land. Second, a constructed house in newly allotted village for lost house will be given.

Status quo compensation package of the government (Money + Site):

Cash will be given on per acre basis, which is fixed based on discussions with farmers of the villages and the prevailing market value of the land. The cash compensation for land lost is different for dry land, single crop irrigated land and complete irrigated land. Cash will be given for their lost house depending up on its valuation done by the committee. The house will be evaluated by the committee formed by the government and will be given cash based on the evaluation. In addition, sites and ex-gratia will be given to construct house, which is based on the land holding on of the farmers. This is given below.

1. Type A Plot (1 Gunta) + Exgratia (Rs. 22000 and 2 major sons of main PDF get 1 site + Rs. 22000 each) for landless people.

2. Type B Plot (2 Guntas) + Exgratia (Rs. 22000 and 2 major sons of main PDF get 1 site + Rs. 22000 each) for farmers with land holding between 25 guntas to 8 acres, 26 guntas.

3. Type C Plot (3Guntas) + Exgratia (Rs. 22000 and 2 major sons of main PDF get 1 site + Rs. 22000 each) for farmers with land holding between 8 acres, 27 guntas to 16 acres, and 26 guntas.

4. Type D Plot (4 Guntas) + Exgratia (Rs. 22000 and 2 major sons of main PDF get 1 site + Rs. 22000 each) for farmers with land holding between 16 acres 27guntas to 25 acres .

5. Type D Plot (4 Guntas) for farmers with land holding more than 25 acres. However, without any exgratia.

In addition, the government is also giving land purchase grant up to Rs. 60000 for those who become landless and marginalized land holder. The stamp duty to purchase the land will be waived off if the farmers buy the land within three years from the date of compensation. It also gives transportation facility to transfer the things from old village to new village.

<u>Self employment trainings includes:</u>

1. Tailoring
2. Packed food preparation like pickles, chips, candies, and durable local food items.
3. Handicraft skills like weaving, wooden toys and gift items, preparing woolen items (like bags, sweaters, mufflers, and caps), leather items preparation (bags, belts, valets, shoes, etc.), etc.
4. Driving vehicles for rent like tractor for cultivation, vehicles for transport, etc.
5. Machinery works like automobiles, local noodle preparing machines, floor grinding chilli powder preparation machines, electricity works, motor winding works, etc.
6. Preparing plantation crops seedlings and seed production methods.
7. Grafting of plantation crops like grapes, lemon and other forest trees like teak wood, Maharani, etc.
8. Cultivation of flowers, vegetables in greenhouse / polyhouse.

HUMBOLDT-UNIVERSITÄT ZU BERLIN

FACULTY OF AGRICULTURE AND HORTICULTURE

Department of Agricultural Economics | Division of Resource Economics | Prof. Dr. Dr. h.c. Konrad Hagedorn

17.01.2016

F.   **Questionnaire: Farmers' Interviews**

Individual Preferences towards Displacement Compensation: A Discrete Choice Approach

Principal Investigator

Mr. Vikram Patil (MSc. Ag)

PhD Scholar

Dept. of Agricultural Economics,

Humboldt University, Berlin.

Email: vikram.patil.1@agrar.hu-berlin.de; vspatil.6@gmail.com

Panel Identification

Code: _____ **Investigator:** _____ **Supervisor:** _____

Date: _____ **Starting Time:** _____ **Ending Time:** _____

Village: _____ **Mandal:** _____ **District:** _____
                              (Taluk)

49. General details

Name of the respondent   :

Age   : _____   Sex (M/F): _____

Education   : _____ (No. of years of schooling)

Occupation   :

Caste   :

Land holding (Acres)   :

(Dry land: _____, Irrigated : _____)

Family Size   : _____

(Male: _____, Female: _____)

Main Source of Income:

☐ Agriculture   ☐ Labor   ☐ Job   ☐ Others

Contact number   :

Suppose you have given below mentioned options of compensation for your land acquisition, how will you rank these alternative options of compensation packages? Assign 1 to the most preferred, 2 to the second most preferred, 3 to third most preferred and continue ranking until 6 being least preferred option.

Choice Set 1: Suppose you become landless

Sl. No	Compensation package	Ranking
1	MONEY + SITE (COMP_PACKAGE_1)	▦
2	MONEY + HOUSE (COMP_PACKAGE_2)	▦
3	LAND + SITE (COMP_PACKAGE_3)	▦
4	LAND + HOUSE (COMP_PACKAGE_4)	▦
5	SELF-EMPLOYMENT + SITE (COMP_PACKAGE_5)	▦
6	SELF-EMPLOYMENT + HOUSE (COMP_PACKAGE_6)	▦

Choice Set 2: Suppose you remain with some land

Sl. No	Compensation package	Ranking
1	MONEY + SITE (COMP_PACKAGE_1)	▦
2	MONEY + HOUSE (COMP_PACKAGE_2)	▦
3	LAND + SITE (COMP_PACKAGE_3)	▦
4	LAND + HOUSE (COMP_PACKAGE_4)	▦
5	SELF-EMPLOYMENT + SITE (COMP_PACKAGE_5)	▦
6	SELF-EMPLOYMENT + HOUSE (COMP_PACKAGE_6)	▦

Thank you very much for spending your valuable time. All the information you have provided will be kept confidential and anonymous and will be used only for research purposes

G. Visual Representations[1]

COMP_PACKAGE_1: <u>Money + Site</u>

This has two components: First, cash will be given for lost land on per acre basis. Second, sites and cash for lost house based on the evaluation by the committee will be given.

1. Cash will be given for lost land on per acre basis

2. One site for main PDF + one site each for two major sons and cash for lost house based on evaluation of the committee will be given.

---

[1] Pictures used are used from various sources like
http://www.123rf.com/photo_9544944_rural-landscape-with-fields.html,
http://articles.economictimes.indiatimes.com/2014-01-23/news/46464132_1_currency-notes-banknotes-central-bank, http://www.annpayscash.com/, and other internet sources.

COMP_PACKAGE_2: <u>Money + House</u>

This has two components: First, Cash will be given for lost land on per acre basis. Second, constructed house in newly allotted village for lost house will be given.

1. Cash will be given for lost land on per acre basis

2. Constructed house in new allotted village will be given and two major sons will get one site each.

COMP_PACKAGE_3: <u>Land + Site</u>

This has two components: First, land will be given for lost land subjected to ceiling (2 acres and remaining cash on per acre basis). Second, sites and cash for lost house based on the evaluation by the committee will be given.

1. Land for land will given subjected to ceiling (2 acres) in any place of the district.

Cash will be given for remaining lost land on per acre basis

2. One site for main PDF + one site each for two major sons and cash for lost house based on evaluation of the committee will be given.

COMP_PACKAGE_4: <u>Land + House</u>

This has two components: First, land will be given for lost land subjected to ceiling (2 acres and remaining cash on per acre basis). Second, constructed house in newly allotted village for lost house will be given.

1. Land for land will given subjected to ceiling (2 acres) in any place of the district.

Cash will be given for remaining lost land on per acre basis

2. Constructed house in new allotted village will be given and two major sons will get one site each.

COMP_PACKAGE_5: <u>Training for self-employment + Site</u>

This has three components: First, training for self-employment with technical and financial assistance for purchase of tools. Second, cash for lost land on per acre basis. Third, sites and cash for lost house based on the evaluation by the committee will be given.

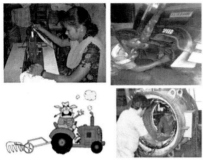

1. Self-employment training with technical and financial assistance to purchase of tools.

2. Cash will be given for lost land on per acre basis

3. One site for main PDF + one site each for two major sons and cash for lost house based on evaluation of the committee will be give

COMP_PACKAGE_6: <u>Training for self employment + House</u>

This has three components: First, training for self employment with technical and financial assistance for purchase of tools. Second, cash for lost land on per acre basis. Third, a constructed house in newly allotted village for lost house will be given.

1. Training for self employment with technical and financial assistance for purchase of tools.

2. Cash will be given for lost land on per acre basis

3. Constructed house in new allotted village will be given and two major sons will get one site each.

Institutional Change in Agriculture and Natural Resources
Institutioneller Wandel der Landwirtschaft und Ressourcennutzung

edited by/herausgegeben von Volker Beckmann & Konrad Hagedorn

Erschienene Bände in der Reihe:

Bd. 1: BREM, Markus, *Landwirtschaftliche Unternehmen im Transformationsprozess: Ein Beitrag zur Theorie der Restrukturierung während des Übergangs vom Plan zum Markt.* 320 S., pb EUR 28,00, ISBN 978-3-8265-8656-9 (1/2001).

Bd. 2: PAVEL, Ferdinand, *Success and Failure of Post-Communist Transition: Theory and an Application to Bulgaria.* 210 S., pb EUR 28,00, ISBN 978-3-8265-8774-0 (2/2001).

Bd. 3: SCHLÜTER, Achim, *Institutioneller Wandel und Transformation: Restitution, Transformation und Privatisierung in der tschechischen Landwirtschaft.* 360 S., pb EUR 28,00, ISBN 978-3-8265-9284-3 (3/2001).

Bd. 4: BOGER, Silke, *Agricultural Markets in Transition: An Empirical Study on Contracts and Transaction Costs in the Polish Hog Sector.* 300 S., pb EUR 28,00, ISBN 978-3-8265-9634-6 (4/2001).

Bd. 5: KLAGES, Bernd: *Die Privatisierung der ehemals volkseigenen landwirtschaftlichen Flächen in den neuen Bundesländern: Grundlagen, Rahmenbedingungen, Ausgestaltung und Wirkungen.* 520 S., pb EUR 38,00, ISBN 978-3-8265-9714-5 (5/2001).

Bd. 6: VERHAEGEN, Ingrid/VAN HUYLENBROECK, Guido: *Hybrid Governance Structures for Quality Farm Products: A Transaction Cost Perspective.* 200 S., pb EUR 28,00, ISBN 978-3-8265-9774-9 (6/2002).

Bd. 7: HURRELMANN, Annette: *Land Markets in Economic Theory: A Review of the Literature and Proposals for Further Research.* 138 S., pb EUR 18,00, ISBN 978-3-8265-9844-9 (7/2002).

Bd. 8: BOGALE, Ayalneh: *Land Degradation, Impoverishment and Livelihood Strategies of Rural Households in Ethiopia: Farmers' Perceptions and Policy Implication.* 236 S., pb EUR 28,00, ISBN 978-3-8322-0214-9 (8/2002).

Bd. 9: ZILLMER, Sabine: *Arbeitsangebotsverhalten im Transformationsprozess: Eine empirische Analyse des polnischen Agrarsektors.* 334 S., pb EUR 28,00, ISBN 978-3-8322-0356-6 (9/2002).

Bd. 10: GATZWEILER, Franz/JUDIS, Renate/HAGEDORN, Konrad: *Sustainable Agriculture in Central and Eastern European Countries: The Environmental Effects of Transition and Needs for Change.* 390 S., pb EUR 28,00, ISBN 978-3-8322-0366-5 (10/2002).

Bd. 11: MILCZAREK, Dominika: *Privatisation as a Process of Institutional Change: The Case of State Farms in Poland.* 154 S., pb EUR 18,00, ISBN 978-3-8322-0364-1 (11/2002).

Bd. 12: CURTISS, Jarmila: *Efficiency and Structural Changes in Transition: A Stochastic Frontier Analysis of Czech Crop Production.* 284 S., pb EUR 28,00, ISBN 978-3-8322-0365-8 (12/2002).

Bd. 13: CLASEN, Ralf: *Jenseits des Sonderfalls: Eine vergleichende Analyse der Agrartransformation in Ostdeutschland und Estland aus der Perspektive des akteurzentrierten Institutionalismus.* 392 S., pb EUR 28,00, ISBN 978-3-8322-1004-5 (13/2002).

Bd. 14: LÜTTEKEN, Antonia: *Agrar-Umweltpolitik im Transformationsprozess: Das Beispiel Polen.* 316 S., pb EUR 28,00, ISBN 978-3-8322-1134-9 (14/2002).

Bd. 15: HANISCH, Markus: *Property Reform and Social Conflict: A Multi-Level Analysis of the Change of Agricultural Property Rights in Post-Socialist Bulgaria.* 322 S., pb EUR 28,00, ISBN 978-3-8322-2093-8 (15/2003).

Bd. 16: GATZWEILER, Franz: *The Changing Nature of Economic Value: Indigenous Forest Garden Values in Kalimanatan, Indonesia.* 250 S., pb EUR 28,00, ISBN 978-3-8322-1973-4 (16/2003).

Bd. 17: LÖW, Daniel: *Crop Farming in China: Technology, Markets, Institutions and the Use of Pesticides.* 242 S., pb EUR 28,00, ISBN 978-3-8322-2373-1 (17/2003).

Bd. 18: VANNOPPEN, Jan/VAN HUYLENBROECK, Guido/VERBEKE, Wim: *Economic Conventions and consumer valuation in specific quality food supply networks.* 202 S., pb EUR 28,00, ISBN 978-3-8322-3065-4 (18/2004).

Bd. 19: KORF, Benedikt: *Conflict, Space and Institutions: Property Rights and the Political Economy of War in Sri Lanka.* 232 S., pb EUR 28,00, ISBN 978-3-8322-3219-1 (19/2004).

Bd. 20: RUDOLPH, Markus: *Agrarstrukturpolitik im vereinten Deutschland: Eine Analyse der Gemeinschaftsaufgabe "Verbesserung der Agrarstruktur und des Küstenschutzes" im Lichte der Neuen Politischen Ökonomie.* 492 S., pb EUR 38,00, ISBN 978-3-8322-3807-0 (20/2005).

Bd. 21: NGUYEN, Tan Quang: *What Benefits and for Whom?: Effects of Devolution of Forest Management in Dak Lak, Vietnam.* 346 S., pb EUR 28,00, ISBN 978-3-8322-3905-3 (21/2005).

Bd. 22: HIDAYAT, Aceng: *Institutional Analysis of Coral Reef Management: A Case Study of Gili Indah Village, West Lombok, Indonesia.* 252 S., pb EUR 28,00, ISBN 978-3-8322-3815-5 (22/2005).

Bd. 23: THEESFELD, Insa: *A Common Pool Resource in Transition: Determinants of Institutional Change for Bulgaria's Postsocialist Irrigation Sector.* 308 S., pb EUR 28,00, ISBN 978-3-8322-3906-0 (23/2005).

Bd. 24: HURRELMANN, Annette: *Agricultural Land Markets: Organisation, Institutions, Costs and Contracts in Poland.* 262 S., pb EUR 28,00, ISBN 978-3-8322-4114-8 (24/2005).

Bd. 25: EGGERS, Jörg: *Dezentralisierung der Agrarumweltmaßnahmen in der europäischen Agrarpolitik: Hemmnisse eines institutionellen Wandels.* 300 S., pb EUR 28,00, ISBN 978-3-8322-4170-4 (25/2005).

Bd. 26: BECKMANN, Volker/HAGEDORN, Konrad: *Understanding Agricultural Transition: Institutional Change and Economic Performance in a Comparative Perspective.* 510 S., pb EUR 38,00, ISBN 978-3-8322-4795-9 (26/2007).

Bd. 27: TRAN, Thanh Ngoc: *From Legal Acts to Village Institutions and Forest Use Practices: Effects of Devolution in the Central Highlands of Vietnam.* 244 S., pb EUR 28,00, ISBN 978-3-8322-4796-6 (27/2005).

Bd. 28: HA, Thuc Vien: *Land Reform and Rural Livelihoods: An Examination from the Uplands of Vietnam.* 364 S., pb EUR 28,00, ISBN 978-3-8322-6908-1 (28/2007).

Bd. 29: DIRIMANOVA, Violeta: *Economic Effects of Land Fragmentation: Property Rights, Land Markets and Contracts in Bulgaria.* 270 S., pb EUR 28,00, ISBN 978-3-8322-6948-7 (29/2008).

Bd. 30: JUNGCURT, Stefan: *Institutional Interplay in International Environmental Governance: Policy Interdependence and Strategic Interaction in the Regime Complex on Plant Genetic Resources for Food and Agriculture.* 280 S., pb EUR 28,00, ISBN 978-3-8322-6974-6 (30/2008).

Bd. 31: BANASZAK, Ilona: *Success and Failure of Cooperation in Agricultural Markets: Evidence from Producer Groups in Poland.* 220 S., pb EUR 28,00, ISBN 978-3-8322-6995-1 (31/2008).

Bd. 32: BEYENE, Fekadu: *Challenges and Options in Governing Common Property: Customary Institutions among (Agro-) Pastoralists in Ethiopia.* 254 S., pb EUR 28,00, ISBN 978-3-8322-6375-1 (32/2008).

Bd. 33: BOENING, Frank: *Accessing Land at the Agricultural Frontier: A Case Study from the Honduran Mosquitia.* 370 S., pb EUR 28,00, ISBN 978-3-8322-6994-4 (33/2008).

Bd. 34: HUNDIE, Bekele: *Pastoralism, Institutions and Social Interaction: Explaining the Coexistence of Conflict and Cooperation in Pastoral Afar, Ethiopia.* 234 S., pb EUR 28,00, ISBN 978-3-8322-6376-8 (34/2008).

Bd. 35: THIEL, Andreas: *Environmental Policy Integration and Water Use Development in the Algarve since Portugal's Accession to the European Union.* 358 S., pb EUR 28,00, ISBN 978-3-8322-8105-2 (35/2009).

Bd. 36: BECKMANN, Volker/DUNG, Nguyen Huu/SHI, Xiaoping/SPOOR, Max/ WESSELER, Justus: *Economic Transition and Natural Resource Management in East and Southeast Asia.* 412 S., pb EUR 38,00, ISBN 978-3-8322-8107-6 (36/2010).

Bd. 37: FARRELL, Katharine N.: *Making Good Decisions Well: A Theory of Collective Ecological Management.* 332 S., pb EUR 28,00, ISBN 978-3-8322-8549-4 (37/2009).

Bd. 38: ARZT, Katja: *Lokale Partizipation und nachhaltige Ressourcennutzung: Eine institutionelle Analyse von Agrar-Umwelt-Foren.* 326 S., pb EUR 28,00, ISBN 978-3-8322-8604-0 (38/2009).

Bd. 39: SCHLEYER, Christian: *Institutioneller Wandel von Meliorationssystemen: Eine vergleichende Studie in Ostdeutschland und Polen.* 332 S., pb EUR 28,00, ISBN 978-3-8322-8726-9 (39/2009).

Bd. 40: WEDAJOO, Aseffa Seyoum: *Microeconomics of Wild Coffee Genetic Resources Conservation in Southwestern Ethiopia: Forest zoning and economic incentives for conservation.* 206 S., pb EUR 28,00, ISBN 978-3-8322-8841-9 (40/2010).

Bd. 41: MARGARIAN, Anne: *Die regionale Spezifität des Agrarstrukturwandels: Eine theoretische und empirische Analyse.* 346 S., pb EUR 28,00, ISBN 978-3-8322-9493-9 (41/2010).

Bd. 42: RAUCHENECKER, Katharina: *Institutioneller Wandel im Bereich Jagd und Wildtiermanagement: Das Beispiel der Jagdgenossenschaften.* 288 S., pb EUR 28,00, ISBN 978-3-8322-9587-5 (42/2010).

Bd. 43: VON BOCK UND POLACH, Carlotta: *Die Bedeutung von Sozialkapital und Netzwerken für die saisonale Migration polnischer Arbeitskräfte nach Deutschland: Am Beispiel des brandenburgischen Spargelanbaus.*
260 S., pb EUR 28,00, ISBN 978-3-8440-0314-7 (43/2011).

Bd. 44: IRAWAN, Evi: *The Effect of Labor Organization on Integrated Pest Management (IPM) Adoption: Empirical Study of Durian and Tangerine Production in Thailand.*
ca. 192 S., pb EUR 28,00, ISBN 978-3-8440-0630-8 (44/2012).

Bd. 45: DENEKE, Tilaye Teklewold: *Water Governance in Amhara Region of Ethiopia: An Institutional Analysis.*
234 S., pb EUR 28,00, ISBN 978-3-8440-0725-1 (45/2012).

Bd. 46: HERNÁNDEZ RIVERA, José: *Analysis of Economic Driving Forces in Crop Protection: A Case Study of Apple Production in the EU.*
184 S. pb EUR 28,00, ISBN 978-3-8440-1137-1 (46/2012)

Bd. 47: SRIGIRI, Srinivasa Reddy: *Institutions of collective action and property rights for natural resource management: Participation of rural households in watershed management initiatives in semi-arid India.*
190 S., pb EUR 28,00, ISBN 978-3-8440-1165-4 (47/2014).

Bd. 48: KIMMICH, Christian: *Networks of Coordination and Conflict: Governing Electricity Transactions for Irrigation in South India.*
198 S., pb EUR 28,00, ISBN 978-3-8440-1947-6 (48/2013).

Bd. 49: CHALIGANTI, Raghu: *Biofuel promotion in India: Analyzing the policy process from a discursive-institutional perspective.*
268 S., pb EUR 28,00, ISBN 978-3-8440-2718-1 (49/2014).

Bd. 50: STUPAK, Nataliya: *Institutional Analysis of Black Earth Soil Degradation and Conservation in Ukraine.*
280 S., pb EUR 28,00, ISBN 978-3-8440-2734-1 (50/2014).

Bd. 51: GHOSH, Ranjan Kumar: *Towards Transaction Cost Regulation: Insights from the Indian Power Generation Sector.*
218 S., pb EUR 28,00, ISBN 978-3-8440-3263-5 (51/2014).

Bd. 52: BISARO, Alexander: *Climate Change Adaptation and Wetlands Governance in Lesotho: A Discourse and Institutional Analysis.*
278 S., pb EUR 28,00, ISBN 978-3-8440-3521-6 (52/2015).

Bd. 53: DAEDLOW, Katrin: *Institutional Change and Persistence in German Recreational-Fisheries Governance in Response to External and Internal Challenges.*
202 S., pb EUR 28,00, ISBN 978-3-8440-3641-1 (53/2015).

Bd. 54: WATANABE, Shigeo: *An Institutional Analysis of Biotrade Contract Implementation: The Case of Namibian Marula Plant Oil.* 294 S., pb EUR 28,00, ISBN 978-3-8440-3780-7 (54/2015).

Bd. 55: BERGER, Lars: *Understanding the Social Construction of Unsustainable Human Behaviour: The Example of Agricultural Non-Point-Source Pollution in Lake Tai, China.* 182 S., pb EUR 28,00, ISBN 978-3-8440-3809-5 (55/2015).

Bd. 56: TAN, Rong: *Governing Farmland Conversion in China: Transactions and Institutional Fit.* 212 S., pb EUR 28,00, ISBN 978-3-8440-3812-5 (56/2015).

Bd. 57: HAMIDOV, Ahmad: *Institutions of Collective Action for Common Pool Resources Management: Conditions for Sustainable Water Consumers Associations in Semi-Arid Uzbekistan.* 216 S., pb EUR 28,00, ISBN 978-3-8440-3922-1 (57/2015).

Bd. 58: MÜLLER, Ulrike: *Unpacking Governance Dilemmas in India's Local Service Delivery System: Cognition, Rationality and Institutions.* 268 S., pb EUR 28,00, ISBN 978-3-8440-4004-3 (58/2015).

Bd. 59: ARÁUZ TORRES, Mario Alberto: *An Institutional Analysis of Forest Resource Uses in Nueva Segovia, Nicaragua.* 212 S., pb EUR 28,00, ISBN 978-3-8440-4053-1 (59/2015).

Bd. 60: CHIDAMBARAM, Bhuvanachithra: *Vehicle emission reduction: An experimental approach for analysing sustainable traffic strategies.* 272 S., pb EUR 28,00, ISBN 978-3-8440-4064-7 (60/2015).

Bd. 61: PATIL, Vikram: *Governing Farmer Rehabilitation and Resettlement in India.* 180 S., pb EUR 28,00, ISBN 978-3-8440-4092-0 (61/2015).